ERATA

p. 9: He that awaketh early to seek her, shall not labor: for he shall find her sitting as his door.

SHOULD READ: …sitting **at** his door.

p. 120: Please with Christ our songs to spare.

SHOULD READ: **Plead** with Christ our **souls** to spare.

p. 122: For He Whom Thou didn't merit to bear, Alleluia.

SHOULD READ: …Whom Thou didst merit to bear.

De Maria Numquam Satis

OF MARY
THERE IS NEVER ENOUGH

OF MARY
THERE IS NEVER ENOUGH

SECOND EDITION

BY

WILLIAM L. BIERSACH

Catholic Treasures
Box 5034
Monrovia, CA 91017

This book is loosely extracted
from a larger unpublished work by the author entitled
WHILE THE EYES OF THE GREAT ARE ELSEWHERE.

All Biblical quotations are from the
Douay-Rheims Bible, Haydock Edition.

© 2002 by William L. Biersach
Published by Catholic Treasures,
Monrovia, California.

First edition: 1995
Second edition: 2002

ISBN: 1-885692-09-9

Printed and bound in the United States of America.

**Please pray for the Coyne family of Ohio
whose generous contribution made this publication possible.**

This book is dedicated to my mother

Elsie K. Biersach

who first taught me how to pray
the Hail Mary.

∞ ∞ ∞

REMEMBER, O most gracious Virgin Mary, that
never was it known that anyone who fled to Thy
protection, implored Thy help, or sought Thy
intercession, was left unaided. Inspired by this
confidence, I fly unto Thee, O Virgin of virgins,
my Mother. To Thee I come, before Thee I stand,
sinful and sorrowful. O Mother of the Word
Incarnate, despise not my petitions, but in Thy
mercy hear and answer me. Amen.

—Saint Bernard of Clairvaux

CONTENTS

† † †

FOREWORD

BY

MARK ALESSIO

Forsake her not, and she shall keep thee:
love her, and she shall preserve thee.
—Proverbs IV:6

∞ ∞ ∞

It may not be apparent from a perusal of the shelves of your average Catholic bookstore, but the twentieth century was a veritable renaissance of writing and study centered on Our Blessed Mother. The year 1900 saw the first of many international Marian Congresses, and the welcome deluge of papers and journals generated by their participants. The first half of the century saw the publication of many fine books about Mary, while the definition of the Dogma of the Assumption in 1950 and the proclamation of the "Marian Year" in 1954 signaled a fresh surge in Marian study and the publication of yet more worthy books about the Mother of God.

When Pope Pius XII exhorted the Catholic world to celebrate the "Marian Year," he requested that "there be held for this purpose appropriate sermons and discourses." Yes, two thousand years after Our Lady was assumed into Heaven, the time had *still* not come to "ease off" on our interest in Mary, for Catholic writers to seek elsewhere for inspiration. *De Maria numquam satis*—"Of Mary, there is NEVER enough!" The eternal, omnipotent God prepared for Himself a *worthy* Mother. A Mother "worthy" to bear God—that fact alone could give us enough grist for a few lifetimes' worth of reflection. God rested in Mary's womb, and subjected Himself to Her. He associated Her in all facets of our Redemption, and honored Her as only a Son Who is God could.

"Enough" of Mary? That would be like scooping a cupful of water from the ocean, and imagining that we've plumbed its depths. All the greatest writings (and there have been many inspired examples) have only skimmed the surface of Her mysteries and, of course, we still gaze at heavenly things "through a glass in an obscure manner" (I Corinthians XII:12). But therein lies the enjoyment. Our Lord sets before us this unique, magnificent creature—Mary, His Masterpiece—and invites us to explore, to learn, to share our findings. If we do not derive *at least* as much pleasure from this pursuit as any archaeologist rooting about in the Valley of the Kings of ancient Egypt, then we've missed the point. Our subject is singular. Our subject is holy. Our subject is beautiful. Our subject is a *treasure,* in the fullest sense of the word. "When one speaks of trade and politics, one soon grows weary," wrote St. John Vienney, "but when one speaks of the Blessed Virgin, the theme is always new."

And yet, the shelves of our Catholic bookstores more often than not fail to do justice to this truth. By the grace of God, there are some Marian classics still in print as of this writing—St. Louis de Montfort's *True Devotion to the Blessed Virgin,* St. Alphonsus Ligouri's *The Glories of Mary,* Fr. Reginald Garrigou-Lagrange's *The Mother of the Savior and Our Interior Life,* St. Peter Julian Eymard's *Our Lady of the Blessed Sacrament,* etc.—and for this we are grateful. However, for the simple reason that "of Mary there is NEVER enough," a new edition of William Biersach's book bearing this very title is a cause for celebration—and I mean a *real* celebration, accompanied by the popping of corks and the optional funny hats and noise-makers. This will become almost ridiculously obvious about a hundred pages from now.

Sadly, fallen mankind has a habit of giving God its "worst." Particularly in our "post-conciliar" landscape, praises to the Mother of God range in quality from the non-existent, to the tepid, to that particularly vile ecumenical brand that gives Mary some praise, but qualifies it to the point of extinction lest it offend those whose own feelings for Her are, well, less than "warm." The twentieth century began with Marian Congresses and successive series of good books about the Holy Virgin. It ended with the phenomenon of desecrated Marian icons being exhibited in museums around the world as "modern art." So, I'll say it again: a new edition of William Biersach's *Of Mary There Is Never Enough* is a cause for celebration. The world is in dire *need* of such public praise of the Mother of God.

I have a special fondness for this small book. I first read it not long after its initial publication while I was making the Total Consecration to Mary according to St. Louis de Montfort. I didn't know William Biersach from Adam back then, but I wrote a brief letter to him in appreciation of his work. Bill replied, and the result is a solid friendship that has grown richer and deeper over the years. Was it Our Lady's doing? Absolutely!

I perceive three motivating ideas behind *Of Mary There Is Never Enough.* I'll summarize them using the author's own words:

1) "The Catholic Faith is a grand adventure. Let us raise the anchor and depart these tepid doldrums. What awaits us over the horizon may surprise us, it may shock us, it may even arouse within our lazy hearts feelings we've never felt before."

2) "Genuine devotion to Our Lady begins with admiration of Her greatness. The more we learn about Her, the more we are awed by all that She is."

3) "If ever there was a crime in this age, it has been the despicable dishonor paid this Woman by

those who would deny Her the prominence that is
rightly Hers."

The three intertwine perfectly. There is an unmis-
takable and infectious sense of "discovery" in this
book. Under Mr. Biersach's command, our ship
navigates the currents of time, and the history of
creation unfolds around us, allowing us to observe
beyond any possibility of doubt that Mary was, indeed, "playing before the Lord" before Time itself
began ticking. We share in the author's "awe of all
that Mary is" by a careful and generous assessment
of Her place in history. And, strangely enough, this
"awe" doesn't cause us to view Our Lady as a re-
mote figure, as some sort of mythological figure,
someone "too interesting" or distant to be true. On
the contrary, we find ourselves irresistibly charmed
by perfect *humanity,* warm and vibrant.

"When you approach the time for reading about
Mary Immaculate," wrote St. Maximilian Kolbe,
"always remember that you are entering into contact
with a living, loving person."

Best of all, we get to share in the "spirited" de-
fense (pun most definitely intended) of Our Lady's
honor, dignity and place as the author combats, with
the "sword of the Spirit" (Ephesians VI:17), the
"despicable dishonor" shown to Mary by an un-
grateful world.

Don't be misled by the slimness of this volume.
Yes, it's compact. So, according to astronomers, is
the matter in a "black hole," which makes it such a

powerful phenomenon. *Of Mary, There Is Never Enough* is entertaining. It's educational. It's challenging. It's not afraid to accept with undiluted appreciation the naked glory of the works of God. It acknowledges, and with gratitude, the sheer grandeur invested in His Mother by Our Lord Jesus Christ, Who established the Fourth Commandment … and takes it *very* seriously!

Yes, by *Jesus Christ.* The prerogatives and position of Mary in the created order are not inventions of imaginative men and women. They are not the doctrinal equivalents of stained-glass windows or sacred oratorios—mere artistic representations of lofty themes. A "Virgin Mary" wasn't created from fragments of Scripture to satisfy some sort of human need for archetypes, whether of Beauty, Purity, or Womanhood. The Truth is more sublime and, paradoxically, more down-to-earth. St. John Eudes wrote, "Whoever sees Jesus sees Mary, and he who sees Mary beholds Jesus!" What manner of Woman can "mother" the Living God? What manner of Woman held her GOD in her arms, and stared into the unfathomable pools of His eyes?—

> And the heart knew without a word
> A strength below all strength had stirred,
> Lifting the Lord of all the word—
> A woman's arm under a child.

So wrote G. K. Chesterton. What kind of a Woman can "mother" God? "Whoever sees Jesus sees Mary." And, like the archetypal pith-helmet-topped explorer of the old black-and-white movie matinee serials, Mr. Biersach leads the search for this Woman, turning the pages of Scripture over carefully as though they were ancient, brittle maps or parchments, and delighting in each precious truth brought to light. Slowly, the picture emerges. Slowly, the sense of wonder rises ... and rises again and again, as we discover that what we thought was a complete pyramid was only the very tip of a larger one, whose base we're still excavating with fascination.

Okay, it's a kaleidoscopic journey at times, for this book is packed solid with wonders. But, as wild as our exploratory trek gets, Captain Biersach never allows his ship to run aground on purely fanciful notions. Doctrinally speaking, what you read in the following pages, you can take to the bank.

Enough. Each word I write delays your departure for a trip you'll want to take more than once. The treasure awaiting you on this trip was hand-picked by the Living God Himself, so you can only imagine its quality, and the sheer number of its many facets. As for its "value" ... for each and every one of us? That is, of course, inestimable. However, in order to creep a bit closer to the answer, let us give the last word to the great Church Father, Doctor and Poet, St. Ephrem of Syria:

> A wonder is Your Mother: The Lord entered her and became a servant; He entered able to speak and He became silent in her; He entered her thundering and His voice grew silent; He entered Shepherd of all; a lamb He became in

her; He emerged bleating.   The womb of Your Mother overthrew the orders ...

The ship sails, the waters are clear, and the only breeze is the fragrant, invigorating breath of the "Mystical Rose." Bon Voyage!

> —Mark Alessio
> Point Lookout, New York
> June 7, 2002
> The Feast of the Sacred Heart

✝✝✝

OF MARY
THERE IS NEVER ENOUGH

1. WHO IS SHE?

He that awaketh early to seek her, shall not labor: for he shall find her sitting as his door.

—Wisdom VI: 15

∞ ∞ ∞

One only need look at a map of North America to see that the landscape is peppered with cities and towns named after the Blessed Virgin Mary. My own metropolis of Los Angeles was originally called *Nuestra Señora Reina de los Angeles*—"Our Lady Queen of the Angels."* Landmarks such as Point Conception also bear reference to Her. Surely She must have held an important place in the lives of the

---

* The full name was actually *El Pueblo de Nuestra Señora Reina de los Angeles de Porciuncula*, but a comprehensive explanation of this colorful bit of historic nomenclature would take us far afield of the topic at hand.

early explorers for them to name so many places with Her in mind rather than after their wives and sweethearts. What kind of amnesia has overtaken us that we no longer understand what so moved the Spaniards, the French, and the Portuguese that they would praise the Blessed Virgin at every turn of coast, river, and mountain range as they explored the New World?

Why, we might ask, are so many chapels, churches, cathedrals, shrines, monasteries, convents, hospitals, orphanages and so on, all over the planet, named after this Woman who never traveled far from Her place of birth, never performed any great miracles in Her lifetime, and is only mentioned in passing in the Bible after the birth of Christ? What is it about Her that captured the devotion of kings and paupers, theologians and simpletons, explorers and blacksmiths, queens and scullery maids, Saints and sinners? Who could She possibly be? Could a myth carry such weight, provoke such ardor, inspire such devotion, and sustain all this momentum over the span of so many centuries?

Of course, there are those who say that we Catholics put too much emphasis on Mary. Some go further and become downright derogatory. It has become fashionable in some circles to question Her Immaculate Conception (a natural consequence of denying the Fall and Original Sin), Her Virginity with respect to Saint Joseph and the birth of Jesus (ditto the collapse of piety), and Her glorious Assumption into Heaven (the loss of the sense of wonder). Such things are reduced to mere legend, stories to fascinate gullible peasants when the Faith was still young. Most people certainly don't call her "Blessed" let alone "Virgin," and one particularly obnoxious fellow comes to mind who once referred to Her as, "Just an incubator, nothing more."

My own quest in this matter began shortly after my return to the Church after a lapse of a dozen years. One of my first commitments was to say the Rosary daily, which brought me face-to-face with Mary's Immaculate Conception, Assumption, and Coronation. Questions were thus raised which demanded answers.

First I contacted a friend of mine, a man who had stayed within Peter's Barque all the while I had been away. A singularly devout man, he married a fine woman and together they raised a family of eight children*, all of them home-schooled. They had been praying that I would find my way clear to God again; and God had heard their prayers. If anyone knew about Our Lady, it had to be my friend, right?

"So tell me about Mary," I said to him. "Who is She? What is Her place in all of this?"

His answer surprised me. "To tell you the truth, I don't know. My family and I say the Rosary together every night, and we certainly observe all Her feasts, but I really don't know much about Her."

---

* Nine as of this edition.

His Faith had been one of simple acceptance, and I appreciated that. But I knew that, for myself, I needed more in the way of knowledge. If my Faith was not founded on rock-sound reason, I ran the risk of falling away again. Not that feelings didn't play their part, but I needed to satisfy my intellect as well.

So I started digging.

What I found overwhelmed me. It was no accident that most of the Catholic Churches in the world are named after the Blessed Virgin Mary. No mere "incubator" was She, but rather the most necessary and remarkable human being ever born. Clearly, She had played a part in my return to the Faith, a critical and essential part that only became obvious after the fact. There was no way I would have understood while the process was in progress, but I came to realize that Mary plays a vital role in the Salvation of every sincere follower of Christ. Every single one.

How sad it is that so many Catholics have been convinced by outsiders that we place "too much emphasis on Mary," and so purged the Faith of all things Marian. In so doing, or rather undoing, we have deprived ourselves of a spiritual resource so powerful and breathtaking as to defy imagination.

Some have capitulated, but not all. Those "old fogies" who remain in the church after Mass, shunned by the modern liturgical specialists, murmuring Hail Mary's amidst the chitter of so many tiny beads, are holding on for dear life to that same Mother bequeathed to us on Calvary:

When Jesus therefore had seen his mother and the disciple standing whom he loved, he saith to his mother: Woman, behold thy son.

After that, he saith to the disciple: Behold thy mother. And from that hour, the disciple took her to his own.

—Saint John XIX: 26-27

That Mary became our Mother at that moment was understood without equivocation by the Fathers of the early Church. That She is still our Mother has been forgotten by many, but the realization is being rekindled all over Christendom as we turn these pages.

It was through Mary that the salvation of the world was begun, and it is through Mary that it must be consummated.

—Saint Louis Marie de Montfort
True Devotion to Mary

Do we dare rediscover what so many Saints understood as a matter of course, or do we choose to follow the lore of the modernists who rip their Rosaries to pieces in their tin pulpits? Should we revel in the darkness, knocking ourselves senseless against the damp walls of cold stone, or do we pursue the drafts of fresh air into the light of day? Can we continue to wallow in the mud of ignorance to please our peers, or does honor and dignity require that we seek the waters of Truth and stand tall in the warmth of the bright and fiery sun? Do we dare to uncover the

Treasure, the Cache buried under the sands of contemporary indifference, the same Trove transported to the New World aboard Spanish galleons, French transports, and Portuguese frigates, carried within the very hearts of the explorers themselves?

Nothing is equal to Mary, nothing but God is greater than Mary ... Every nature is created by God and God is born of Mary. God created all things and Mary gave birth to God. God who made all things made Himself from Mary and thus He remade everything He had made ... God is the Father of created things and Mary is the Mother of recreated things. God is therefore the Father of the constitution of all things and Mary is the Mother of the restoration of all things. God begot Him through whom all things were made and Mary brought forth Him through whom all things were saved.

Saint Anselm
Opera Omnia

Awaken, Church Militant! To the oars! (Orchestral flourish here.) The Catholic Faith is a grand adventure. Let us raise the anchor and depart these tepid doldrums. What awaits us over the horizon may surprise us, it may shock us, it may even arouse within our lazy hearts feelings we've never felt before.

What have we got to lose?

Our souls! Do you hear? Our very souls!

To the oars, to the oars!

2. THE EYES OF GOD

It is strange that when all attention is upon Christ's humanity and away from his divinity, his Mother should be so pointedly omitted—Events don't have mothers, nor do Meanings! I mention her here as an illustration of the way in which the atmosphere of our world seeps into us without our noticing. I wonder if that could be the reason why she is not much mentioned among ourselves: I cannot remember when I last heard a sermon about her.

—Frank Sheed
What Difference Does Jesus Make?

∞ ∞ ∞

Who is Mary? Why, the Mother of Jesus, of course. Ah, and who indeed was He? To understand Mary, we must understand Him, and to do that we must return to "square one."

Whenever we feel inundated by the sheer immensity of God's goodness, or overwhelmed by the complexities of the veritable latticework which is the Catholic Faith, or simply tired of trying to cram so much information into our hungry but limited minds, it is always consoling to return to the most important question ever asked. It is an ongoing source of strength, courage, refreshment, and honor, because when we tackle "square one," the question He Himself asked—

> But whom do you say that I am?
> —Saint Matthew XVI:15

—we're renewing our belief, polishing our resolve, reminding ourselves that when Isaias proclaimed the following prophecy—

> Take courage, and fear not: behold your God will bring the revenge of recompense: God himself will come and save you.
> Then shall the eyes of the blind be opened, and the ears of the deaf shall be unstopped.
> Then shall the lame man leap as a hart, and the tongue of the dumb shall be free: for waters are broken out in the desert, and streams in the wilderness.
> —Isaias XXXV: 4-6

—he was speaking of this very same man, Jesus Christ: "God Himself will come and save you." Jesus Christ was God Incarnate, God who came among us because ...

... God so loved the world, as to give his only begotten Son; that whosoever believeth in him, may not perish, but may have life everlasting.

—Saint John III: 16

So, having answered this fundamental question to our satisfaction and His, as did Saint Peter—

Thou art Christ, the Son of the living God.
—Saint Matthew XVI: 16

—we might proceed to the next question, "What was Jesus like?" Would He be indistinguishable from other men? When He was just a baby, didn't He look and behave just like any ordinary infant? Most people these days assume this to be the case, and are indeed adamant about it. Such glib conjecture only demonstrates how far we have descended into the swill of mediocre thinking.

The "silver screen" and the "boob tube" have had a profound and personal impact on our generation, more than any of us would feel comfortable admitting. Even with all the technical advancements of the genre, Hollywood casting directors can only provide ordinary human infants for their otherwise lavish "Life of Christ" productions. Concurrently, modern scholars have for years been freely running with the absurd idea that Jesus wasn't even aware of His own divinity until His Crucifixion. As is their custom, they present their groundless speculations as revealed truths that His "God-consciousness" was submerged within His humanity until He reached adulthood, and that it then rose gradually from subconsciousness to full awareness as His public ministry progressed. As they have done to promote their other agendas, they over-emphasize one passage out of context:

> Before the festival day of the Pasch, Jesus knowing that his hour was come, that he should pass out of this world to the Father: having loved his own who were in the world, he loved them unto the end.
>
> And when supper was done (the devil having now put it into the heart of Judas Iscariot, the son of Simon, to betray him,)
>
> Knowing that the Father had given him all things into his hands, and that he came from God, and goeth to God;
>
> He riseth from supper ...
>
> —Saint John XIII: 1-4

Because of the emphasis here on Jesus "knowing His hour had come" and that "He came from God," they suggest that He somehow didn't know who He was before this moment. In other words, God was capable of suffering from an identity crisis. They conveniently ignore another incident that occurred when He was only twelve years old, when He became separated from His parents:

> And it came to pass, that, after three days, they found him in the temple, sitting in the midst of the doctors, hearing them, and asking them questions.

And all that heard him were astonished at his wisdom and answers.

And seeing him, they wondered. And his mother said to him: Son, why hast thou done so to us? Behold thy father and I have sought thee sorrowing.

And he said to them: How is it that you sought me? Did you not know, that I must be about my father's business?

—Saint Luke II: 46-49

His father's business? Do we honestly think He was promoting Joseph's carpentry enterprise in the temple that day? This is hardly the response of a Child who doesn't know who He is or what He's about. And we can be fairly sure that a Man who goes around saying—

Amen, amen I say to you, before Abraham was made, I am.

—Saint John VIII: 58

—has a clear perception of His own divinity; enough to risk being stoned for it. What the modernists have tried to promote with the unwitting, and in some cases more than willing, aid of star-studded Hollywood celluloid, is the idea that Jesus was in all respects "ordinary." The contemporary mind has lost all sense of awe and propriety, and so perpetually seeks to bring all that is sublime down to its own tacky level. We, having been born and raised in this malaise, are most surely influenced by it. But all is not lost. We can stir the ashes of our dim imaginations and coax the embers back into a roaring blaze.

Like other men, he began at the beginning—an embryo. Like the rest of us, he was born a baby, grew into a small boy, a big boy, a youth, a man. Human bodies have laws, and his was subject to them ...

In other words, he did not take short cuts! He did not use the divinity of his person to bypass the difficulties of his humanity. As an infant, he had to be fed from his mother's breast. He could have nourished his infant body by an act of his divine omnipotence, but that would have been to turn his humanity, not into a farce, but to some extent into a fiction. Miracles, when he came to work them, were for others, not to save himself trouble.

—Frank Sheed
To Know Christ Jesus

How Jesus Christ could be True God and True Man is a great Mystery, and a Mystery well worth grappling with. We should not discard it or bypass it just because it is beyond us, nor should we ever assume that our conclusions are the last word. We must always defer in the end to the dogmatic, infallible pronouncements of Popes and Œcumenical councils:

For we do not say that the nature of the Word was changed and made flesh, nor yet that it was changed into the whole man (composed) of soul and body but rather (we say) that the Word uniting with Himself according to person is a body animated by a rational soul, marvelously and incomprehensibly was made man, and was the Son of man, not according to the will alone or by the assumption of a person alone, but that out of both in one Christ and Son, not because distinction of natures was destroyed by the union, but rather because the divine nature and the human nature formed one Lord and Christ and Son for us, through a marvelous and mystical concurrence in unity ... For in the first place no common man was born of the holy Virgin; then the Word thus descended upon him; but being united from the womb itself he is said to have endured a generation in the flesh in order to appropriate the producing of His own body. Thus [the holy Fathers] did not hesitate to speak of the holy Virgin as the Mother of God.

—Council of Ephesus, 431 AD
"The Incarnation" (Denzinger: 111a)

Well, well, well: "For in the first place *no common man* was born of the Holy Virgin." When the Word became flesh, when the eternal and infinite God took on the skin, muscle, and bone of man, the product could not have been ordinary. So let us try something new, at least, new to us (the idea itself is ancient): let us set aside all mundane expectations. Let us allow ourselves, rather, the opportunity to embrace the *extraordinary.* Let us begin by imagining the Baby Jesus, not as the drooling, writhing, whimpering baby pictured in all the "Life of Christ" movies, but rather as something quite different than what we would expect from a typical newborn.

Let us envision ourselves as one of the shepherds, holding the Christ Child in our arms, bundled in the simple wrapping of poverty. Feel His weight in our hands, the texture of His blanket, the heat of His tiny body penetrating through the cloth, warming the skin of our encompassing arms. Smell the stable straw, hear the crickets chirping outside, sense the evening chill on our cheeks, make the moment as vivid as possible. We look down at His face and into His eyes; and we see not the blank clueless orbs we would expect of a typical newborn, but *the deep, comprehending, riveting consciousness of God looking up at us out of clear, cognizant eyes.* The infinite and omnipotent God Who made the heavens and the earth, Who caused all things to be, Who sustains our very existence from moment to moment by an act of His Divine Will, Who is without beginning or end, without boundary or limits—*God locks eyes with us!*

Imagine *that.* Imagine looking into a mere baby's eyes and seeing *that* looking back at us. It's enough to make the hairs on the back of our necks rise with a terrified shiver. The sheer impossibility of such a thing, and the compounding wonder of its obvious actuality, could easily bring any sane person to the brink of horror. It would be easier to imagine opening a can of beans and finding the known universe slowly swirling around inside. This Child is … *God.* These tiny fingers are flexed by the Mind of God, and those wee lips are curled into a smile of confident recognition by the Will of God, because this Baby knows more about us than we know about ourselves, including the numbers of hairs on our heads, cells in our bodies, secrets in our hearts, and stains on our souls. With a mere thought He could annihilate the world, or rewrite the physical laws that order matter, space, and time.

This fragile Child is HE WHO IS.

With this realization turning like the gyre of an immense hurricane in our minds, let us turn in our imagination to the Mother who just handed us this Child: the Woman who carried Him within Her womb for nine months, who will caress Him in Her arms and nourish Him at Her breast, who will protect Him from harm, who will love Him with a Mother's Love. How could She not know exactly who He is?—and all the while knowing without the slightest fear, alarm or anxiety?

And the shepherds returned, glorifying and praising God, for all the things they had heard and seen …

—Saint Luke II: 20

What kind of a Woman could possibly be the Mother of this Child? To even suggest that an ordinary woman could handle such a task is to mock the intellect. Reason dictates that She had to be special indeed.

So, having first asked and answered, "Whom do you say that I am?" and then, "What was Jesus like?" we are inexorably drawn to the third inevitable question: "And who is His Mother?"

When the Angel Gabriel first appeared to the Blessed Virgin, he addressed Her in a way so unique we must pause and consider his words. The title he bestowed upon Her had never been used before, nor would ever be used thereafter, with respect to a descendent of Adam and Eve:

> And the angel being come in, said unto her: Hail, full of grace, the Lord is with thee: blessed art thou among women.
>
> —Saint Luke I: 28

Since the Fall, no man or woman had been conceived in any state other than Original Sin, void of Grace. When the Angel Gabriel dubbed Her "Full of Grace," he was proclaiming that She was miraculously unique, set apart from every other human creature.

Mary's Full-of-Grace-ness was no trivial or metaphorical matter. The human soul is as real as the blood coursing through our veins; Original Sin is as real as a diseased kidney that ravages the integrity of our circulatory system; and Mary's being born free of the disease is as real as dialysis. Her being "Full of Grace" was absolutely necessary for the completion of the purpose for which She had been called.

In the Old Testament, the symbol of God's presence among the people of Israel was the *Shekinah*, or visible holy light, which filled the tabernacle where the Ark of the Covenant resided.

The cloud covered the tabernacle of the testimony, and the glory of the Lord filled it.

Neither could Moses go into the tabernacle of the covenant, the cloud covering all things and the majesty of the Lord shining, for the cloud had covered all.

—Exodus XL: 32-33

This indwelling of the Spirit of God was no mere optical illusion, but was as real as real can be; as was discovered by an unfortunate man by the name of Oza during the time of King David. The Ark of the Covenant was being transported on an oxcart, amidst a joyous procession led by David himself. The people were singing hymns and playing instruments, but the festivities were suddenly interrupted:

And when they came to the floor of Chidon, Oza put forth his hand, to hold up the ark: for the ox being wanton had made it lean a little on one side.

And the Lord was angry with Oza, and struck him, because he had touched the ark; and he died there before the Lord.

And David was troubled because the Lord had divided Oza: and he called that place the Breach of Oza to this day.

—I Paralipomenon XIII: 9-11

Why was Oza struck dead—not just struck but "divided," split, torn asunder—just for trying to steady the Ark so it wouldn't fall? Because the indwelling power of the Holy Ghost was *incompatible* with man in his sinful state, no matter the man's good intention.

The Angel Gabriel told Mary:

> The Holy Ghost shall come upon thee, and the power of
> the most High shall overshadow thee. And therefore also
> the Holy which shall be born of thee shall be called the
> Son of God.
>
> —Saint Luke I: 35

The same holy and lethal *Shekinah* that had over-shadowed the Ark of the Convenant would come upon Mary. Thus Jesus Christ would be conceived in Her womb. If She Herself had not been immaculately conceived and was therefore free from Original Sin when the Spirit of God indwelled in Her, She would have *died.*

> In the knowledge of these exalted mysteries and decrees,
> I confess myself ravished in admiration and transported
> beyond my proper self. Perceiving this most holy and
> pure Creature formed and conceived in the divine mind
> from the beginning and before all ages, I joyously and ex-
> ultingly magnify the Omnipotent for the admirable and
> mysterious decree, by which He formed for us such a pure
> and grand, such a mysterious and godlike Creature, worthy
> rather to be admired and praised by all beings, than to be
> described by any one …
>
> … I am ravished in the perception of this tabernacle of
> God, and I perceive that the Author of it is more admirable
> in her creation, than in that of all the rest of the world, al-
> though the diversity of the creatures manifests the wonder-
> ful power of their Creator. In this Queen alone are com-
> prehended and contained more treasures than in all the rest

of things joined together, and the variety and preciousness of her riches honor the Lord above all the multitudes of the other creatures.

> —Sister Mary of Jesus of Agreda
> "The Conception"
> *Mystical City of God*

If these concepts shock us, then we would do well to take some time and give them serious consideration. Perhaps when we asked, "And who is His Mother?" we were not prepared for so long, glorious, ponderous, and expansive an answer, but that (in the most specific and realistic sense of the maxim) is Life. If the whole thing seems alien, then we must see ourselves in the context of a culture that steers us away from such exalted ideas at every turn. If we were not taught these things by those that should have done so, then we begin to see how successful the modernist attack on the Faith has been. So where do we go from here?

If we are to do our duty to Christ the King, we must accept the challenge of Catholic reconstruction. To do that, we must each of us acquire the education denied us. We could not help being robbed; we can blame only ourselves if we remain poor.

> —Charles A. Coulombe
> *Everyman Today Call Rome*

There is no excuse for remaining poor. The Old Knowledge is still available, it just takes a little searching. Let us look further.

† † †

3. THE TIME BEFORE TIME

The Lord possessed me in the beginning of his ways, before he made any thing from the beginning.

I was set up from eternity, and of old before the earth was made.

—Proverbs VIII: 22-23

∞ ∞ ∞

We must open our minds to a Great Secret. We must do our best to transcend the limits of our carnal perceptions to understand, or begin to understand, this most awesome mystery: Mary was in the Mind of God from the very beginning, from *before* the very beginning.

How can this be?

God does not exist in time. There is no time, as we know it, for God. Time is a created thing, as is space and matter. It was made as a vehicle or medium within which we live and move. But He is not bound by it, any more than He is confined by His universe. To God there is no past or future; the first beat of our

heart and the final exhale of breath are *now*. The Fall
of Adam is as present to Him as the blowing of the
last trumpet in the Apocalypse. We experience time
in a continuous line, as a series of sequential events.
He perceives all time and events in the eternal Now.

Bearing this is mind, we turn to the book of Proverbs in the Old Testament. From within its seemingly loose frame of parables and similitudes there
emerges an interesting theme. Wisdom, which at first
is described as a desirable virtue—

> If wisdom shall enter into thy heart, and knowledge
> please thy soul:
> Counsel shall keep thee, and prudence shall preserve
> thee ...

Proverbs II: 10-11

—gradually takes on seemingly human traits—

> Say to wisdom: Thou art my sister: and call prudence
> thy friend ...

—Proverbs VII: 4

—and finally develops into an actual personality,
Wisdom Personified:

> I wisdom dwell in counsel, and am present in learned
> thoughts.
> The fear of the Lord hateth evil: I hate arrogance, and
> pride, and every wicked way, and a mouth with a double
> tongue.

—Proverbs VIII: 12-13

Here, if we only have eyes to see, is where Mary emerges as a thought in the Mind of God, a thought which He held before the world began. The Church Fathers understood, as must we: Mary's mystical name within the ebb and flow of Old Testament prophecy is WISDOM. Thus the Church applies the words that follow to Her, as the thought of Mary speaking of Herself from outside of time:

The Lord possessed me in the beginning of his ways, before he made any thing from the beginning.

I was set up from eternity, and of old before the earth was made.

The depths were not as yet, and I was already conceived, neither had the fountains of waters as yet sprung out:

The mountains with their huge bulk had not as yet been established: before the hills I was brought forth:

He had not yet made the earth, nor the rivers, nor the poles of the world.

When he prepared the heavens, I was present: when with a certain law and compass he enclosed the depths:

When he established the sky above, and poised the fountains of waters:

When he encompassed the sea with its bounds, and set a law to the waters that they should not pass their limits: when he balanced the foundations of the earth;

I was with him forming all things: and was delighted every day, playing before him at all times;

Playing in the world: and my delights were to be with the children of men.

—Proverbs VIII: 22-31

This is not to say that Mary pre-existed Herself, but that God's thought of Her was so real, so complete, so loving, that it was as if the very thought of Her could sing and play, and indeed, could already demonstrate care and concern for the hearts of men, those who would one day be Her children. What power permeates these words when we perceive them issuing from Her most pure and maternal mouth:

> Now therefore, ye children, hear me: Blessed are they that keep my ways.
>
> Hear instruction and be wise, and refuse it not.
>
> Blessed is the man that heareth me, and that watcheth daily at my gates, and waiteth at the posts of my doors.
>
> He that shall find me, shall find life, and shall have salvation from the Lord:
>
> But he that shall sin against me, shall hurt his own soul. All that hate me love death.
>
> —Proverbs VIII: 32-36

Mary, then, is not just an historical nobody we can ignore. She is a vibrant, powerful, integral, and compelling part of the unfolding story of the Salvation of Mankind. "He that shall find me, shall find life, and shall have salvation from the Lord"—a beautiful promise of hope to those who are open to Her message. "All that hate me love death"—sobering words for those who would relegate Her to the status of a mere "incubator" or worse.

Thus, before all other creatures, was She conceived in the divine mind, in such manner and such state as befitted and became the dignity, excellence and gifts of the humanity of her most holy Son. To her flowed over, at once and immediately, the river of the Divinity and its attributes with all its impetuosity, in as far as a mere creature is capable and as is due to the dignity of the Mother of God.

—Sister Mary of Jesus of Agreda
"The Conception"
Mystical City of God

Before God made the Angels—"before" being a concession to the limitations of our language—He knew a third of them would turn away. Before He made Adam, He knew the first man would fall. Before all time, God knew His Son would become a Man to rectify the situation. He knew He would require a human woman for a spouse so that He could enter human history. Having assumed the humble form of a helpless Child, He would then need the assistance and ministrations of a Mother. And for any of this to be accomplished, He first required a Woman who loved Him enough to obey Him without question, with complete trust; a Woman who would be His Handmaid.

She originated on this little planet of ours, pertains to our race, our kind, is related to us not by angelic ties of love and thought, but by the very fibres of flesh and blood.

Her alliance to God is threefold. She is the Daughter of the Father, the Spouse of the Holy Spirit, and the Mother of the Son. She presents all creation with a baby, whose name in Eternity is God, and whose name in time is Jesus.

—Father Leonard Feeney
You'd Better Come Quietly

No other human being has ever had, or could ever have, such a "tri-lationship" with God. What other woman in all history possessed within herself the obedience, humility and purity necessary to be the Daughter and Handmaid of God, accepting His Will and Plan without question, hesitation, or comprehension of the consequences?

What other woman was spotless, pure, perfect enough to receive the Holy Ghost as Her intimate Spouse? In Her womb the Human and the Divine combined to form the Body of the Son of God. Within Her very body, the incomprehensibility of the Blessed Trinity became inexorably entwined with the mystery of the Incarnation, the very notion of which could engulf the human mind for a lifetime of meditation and wonder:

The Holy Ghost willed and operated that from Her would be conceived and born He from whom He Himself proceeded.

—Saint Anselm
De concep. vrig.

No one could "look down" at the vulnerable humanity of Jesus Christ more intimately than Mary

His Mother as she held Him in Her arms. She nursed Him, clothed Him, saw to His physical needs when He was a defenseless infant.

In this light, do not the reverent words of a Saint make far more sense than the mediocre rendition handed to us on paper plates by the modernists?

> In my admiration I can say with St. Dionysius the Areopagite: "If faith would not instruct me, and if the understanding of what I see would not teach me, that is God, who has conceived Her in his mind, and who alone could and can in his Omnipotence form such an image of his Divinity, if all this were not present to my mind, I might begin to doubt, whether the Virgin Mother contain not in Herself Divinity."
>
> —Sister Mary of Jesus of Agreda
> "The Conception"
> *Mystical City of God*

If the flowery language is a "bit much" for our twenty-first century taste, we would do well to remember that ours is the culture that caters to the lowest common element of society. Ours is the culture that over-humanizes Christ at the expense of His Divinity. Ours is the culture that celebrates the mediocre, panders the trivial, and promotes the vulgar. Yet ours is the culture that looks back on the past with disdain, as if our ancestors lacked our "class." Truly, we don't know the meaning of the word.

Another word that eludes us is "Universals." The rampant relativism of our age has all but eradicated this concept from our minds—a concept that for centuries was the philosophical foundation of Catholic thinking and understanding. We, as sincere Catholics, would do well to reinstate it in our vocabularies:

> The Church Fathers looked primarily to Plato as the foremost Greek philosopher. He first proposed the idea of "Universals," that is of ideal prototypes of things like "Man" and "Horse," as well as abstract qualities like "Love" and "Honor." These Plato held to exist in some "realm of the Types" whence they cast reflections on our poor earth. We ourselves, for instance, are mere reflections of the great archetype "Man," of whose substance we all partake—hence our "mannishness."
>
> … Christian philosophers deduced that these "types" did not exist in some kingdom of their own, but in the mind of God. They were no less real for all of that; in a certain sense they were more real than those of their reflections which were soul-less (rocks, etc.). Further, these archetypes share the timelessness of God—for He has thought of them for all eternity. So applying this idea to the Old Testament, they found, that just as the Holy Ghost—the *Shekinah* … had existed from all eternity … so too had the Son, the divine *Logos,* although not yet incarnate. Similarly, from all eternity was Our Lady, the vessel whereby the Logos became flesh, present in the mind of God as the figure of Wisdom, of *Sophia.*
>
> —Thomas A. Hutchinson
> *Desire and Deception*

"Be that as it may," says the skeptic, "you certainly can't base this supra-temporal in-the-Mind-of-God Mariology on a few verses from the Book of Proverbs."

Most certainly not. We have much ground yet to cover. Let us first deal with the Ultimate Verse, the majestic pinnacle from which all the rivers of prophecy flow ...

4. THE SQUARE
BEFORE SQUARE ONE

Inimicitias ponam inter te et mulierem, et semen tuum
et semen illius.

Ipsa conteret caput tuum, et tu insidiaberis calcaneo
eius.

—Genesis III: 15
The Latin Vulgate

∞ ∞ ∞

Okay, from the top—or rather, this time we will
take it from a point *preceding* the top. Let us go
back, way back, all the way back to "the square *be-fore* square one." Can there be such a place? Most
assuredly so. We can never become complacent in
the Land of the Faith. There is always another adventure awaiting us, if we but seek it out.

As we have seen, the most significant question ever
asked in the history of the world was, "Whom do
you say that I am?" But proceeding from this pivotal
query is yet another question regarding an event that

preceded it by five thousand years: "Whom do you say *She* is?"

If we run our eyes back up the page, we find just under the chapter heading a Treasure Map disguised as a verse from the Latin Vulgate. (Treasure hunters take note: "X marks the spot"—or in this case, "Ipsa.") This particular verse is so important that it has been given its own name. It is called the *Protoevangelium,* which means the "First Good News." It is the first of all prophecies, pronounced by God Himself in the Garden of Eden. A sound case could be made that it is the most important verse in the entire Bible because all the great, wonderful, and awesome things that are to follow—the history of the Israelites, the line of descent of the patriarchs, the coming of the prophets, even the commission of Jesus Christ in His First and Second Comings—are essentially contained within it. And, curiouser and curiouser, this prophecy is addressed to, of all people, the serpent who had just succeeded in luring Adam and Eve into the pit of Sin. Let us consider this verse ever so carefully:

> I will put enmities between thee and the woman, and thy seed and her seed:
>
> She shall crush thy head, and thou shalt lie in wait for her heel.
>
> —Genesis III: 15
> *The Douay-Rheims Translation*

Here we find two distinct statements. First, that the lines of battle have been drawn: on one side stands "the woman" and "her seed," on the other, Satan and his minions. Second, that the outcome of the conflict has already been determined: "she" will conquer, while Satan's defeat is deemed inevitable.

On first reading, one might assume that "the woman" is obviously Eve, and that "her seed" refers to her offspring, the human race; but as we shall see, something far more profound is at work here. This is not, as so many faithless "experts" suggest, just the moral of a fairy tale, a quaint mythological explanation for the general human aversion to things that slither on the ground. We must bear in mind that Moses, the author of Genesis, was inspired by the Holy Ghost, that God preserved this information for thousands of years specifically for our benefit, and that we have a mandate from Jesus Christ Himself to seek out and grasp its significance:

> For if you did believe Moses, you would perhaps believe me also; for he wrote of me.
>
> But if you do not believe his writings, how will you believe my words?
>
> —Saint John V: 46-47

Our quest for the Truth dies here if we do not take these words of Christ seriously. As often as we have returned to "square one," we should begin to understand this by now. God Incarnate warns us that we will not comprehend His mission if we discount the writings of Moses. If we are still clinging to the vestiges of the theory of evolution, we will have to cut them loose. The *Protoevangelium* is absolute and specific. The identity of the "woman" in Genesis III: 15 is not a matter for idle speculation over cocktails. Her identity is crucial to our understanding of everything else, including "square one."

So back to this "woman." Let us take note: nowhere else in the Bible is "seed" attributed to a woman, for "seed" is something exclusively male. Very strange indeed. As for this "woman" who will defeat Satan, could she possibly be Eve, the same Eve who just moments before stumbled so easily into the clutches of the father of lies? Unlikely—not without some instant, dramatic change in her character. Besides, God had other plans for Eve's destiny, punishments described in the very next verse:

> I will multiply thy sorrows, and thy conceptions: in sorrow shalt thou bring forth children, and thou shalt be under thy husband's power, and he shall have dominion over thee.

> —Genesis III: 16

But, we may ask, if Eve was the only woman on earth at the time the *Protoevangelium* was uttered, who could "the woman" possibly be? We must remind ourselves that to God there is no time. In the Mind of God, Mary, daughter of Joachim and Anne fifty centuries hence, was already "playing before him at all times." The Woman of Genesis is none other than Mary, the Virgin who would miraculously bear a Son, not with the participation of a human male, but by the power of the Holy Ghost. Her "seed" is none other than Jesus Christ.

The conflict described in the *Protoevangelium,* then, is twofold. Enmities were put between "thee and the woman," that is, between Satan and Mary; and also between "thy seed and her seed," between the hoards of Hell and Jesus Christ. The war over the Salvation of Mankind is not just between God and Satan, but involves Mary as well. More than merely drawn into the struggle, She is *pivotal.* It is She that will ultimately "crush thy head." God in His Wisdom deemed that the defeat of Satan will be accomplished, not by a mighty army, nor even by the Hand of His Only Begotten Son, but by the heel of His lowly Handmaid.

> God has never made and formed but one enmity; but it is an irreconcilable one, which shall endure and grow even to the end. It is between Mary, His worthy Mother, and the devil—between the children and servants of the Blessed Virgin, and the children and tools of Lucifer. The most terrible of all the enemies which God has set up against the devil is His holy Mother Mary. He has inspired her, even since the days of the earthly paradise—though she existed then only in His idea—with so much hatred against that cursed enemy of God, with so much ingenuity in unveiling the malice of that ancient serpent, with so much power to conquer, to overthrow and to crush that proud, impious rebel, that he fears her not only more than

all angels and men, but in a sense more than God Himself. Not that the anger, the hatred, and the power of God are not infinitely greater than those of the Blessed Virgin, for the perfections of Mary are limited; but first, because Satan, being proud, suffers infinitely more from being beaten and punished by a little and humble handmaid of God, and her humility humbles him more than the divine power; and secondly, because God has given Mary such great power against the devils that—as they have often been obliged to confess, in spite of themselves, by the mouths of the possessed—they fear one of her sighs for a soul more than the prayers of all the saints, and one of her threats against them more than all other torments.

—Saint Louis Marie de Montfort
True Devotion to Mary

If the mind boggles, let it. There's nothing like a good boggling to stir up the ol' gray matter. What we must *not* do is dismiss this crucial point simply because it is new to us, or beyond us, or because our Protestant "brethren" balk at its implications. Understanding the ramifications of the *Protoevangelium* is more important today, as the twenty-first century commences to grind its way through the gears, than at any other time in history. Why? It is crucial that we, the Church Militant, comprehend from a tactical standpoint that even though Her Son is God Incarnate, it is not He but She who is destined to crush Satan in the end.

It was through Mary that the salvation of the world was begun, and it is through Mary that it must be consummated ...

It is principally of these last and cruel persecutions of the devil, which shall go on increasing daily till the reign of Antichrist, that we ought to understand the first and celebrated prediction and curse of God pronounced in the terrestrial paradise against the serpent ...

> —Saint Louis Marie de Montfort
> *True Devotion to Mary*

This attention on Mary in no way lessens the role or the power of Jesus Christ. Indeed, just the opposite, for God's unique *modus operandi* is becoming familiar to us:

But the foolish things of the world hath God chosen, that he may confound the wise: and the weak things of the world hath God chosen, that he may confound the strong.

> —I Corinthians I: 27

Thus He takes delight in defeating Satan by means of His Blessed Mother. God could fight the battle, but—how grand!—He prefers that the army be led by an unexpected general ...

... because Satan, being proud, suffers infinitely more from being beaten and punished by a little and humble handmaid of God ...

> —Saint Louis Marie de Montfort
> *True Devotion to Mary*

Let us share His delight, luxuriating in the Divine Irony. How marvelous and gracious is God that He would so bless His children. The promise of God, declared at the dawn of time and preserved through the ages, roars down through the centuries to engulf our hearts today with the fire of hope, courage, and solace. One cannot overstate the importance of the *Protoevangelium* and its significance to us in the here and now: *the war is won, the devil is defeated, the victory is Hers, and we share in Her triumph.* On this we can depend, on this we can hang our very souls.

In the immediate and personal sense, however, it may appear that the battle is not going our way. In point of fact, you and I may go down in smoke. The way things are going, it is not outside the realm of possibility that we will end our lives in martyrdom. To carnal eyes, what surer sign of defeat is there than execution? If we despair in our own predicament, we fall to the side of the serpent who wants nothing more than to draw us under the shadow of Our Blessed Mother's heel to share in his eternal demise. But if we clutch the truth of the First Good News to our hearts, marching forth in confidence under Mary's banner, we will share in Her conquest. This should be our lively hope ...

> ... Unto an inheritance incorruptible, and undefiled, and that can not fade, reserved in heaven for you.
>
> —I Saint Peter I: 4

This is the stuff of Faith: that we rely not on the input of our senses but on the promises of God. As with the Transubstantiation, we believe according to the command of Christ rather than the data relayed through our optic nerves and taste buds. It follows that our hope is of a similar disposition. No matter what befalls us, no matter how bleak things may seem; even as the very life is drained from our bodies through the punctures of the serpent's deadly fangs, we have this eternal hope, this promise on which to cling. Those who fall in battle in service to the cause nonetheless share in the glories of the final victory. Those who side with the Woman of Genesis will cheer as She crushes Satan under her humble but mighty heel. And the reward for our loyalty cannot be measured by the currency of this world, for our sights are not here but elsewhere.

> Blessed shall you be when men shall hate you, and when they shall separate you, and shall reproach you, and cast out your name as evil, for the Son of man's sake.
> Be glad in that day and rejoice; for behold, your reward is great in heaven. For according to these things did their fathers to the prophets.
>
> —Saint Luke VI: 22-23

✝✝✝

5. THE SERPENT CRUSHED

He was a murderer from the beginning, and he stood not
in the truth; because truth is not in him. When he speaketh a lie, he speaketh of his own: for he is a liar, and the
father thereof.

—Saint John VIII: 44

∞ ∞ ∞

So significant is the ancient prophecy of the
Protoevangelium, such a consolation to us who roam
the fields of battle today, that Satan has done everything in his power to obfuscate its meaning, to rob the
Church Militant of our rightful hope, courage, and
solace. No other verse in the Bible has come under
more scrutiny and attack, not just by those outside the
Barque of Peter, but in recent times by the modernist
termites who have infested the hull.

The why is obvious: to deprive us of access to a
Conduit of infinite Grace, to break our spirit, to shat-
ter our confidence, to call into question that which we
hold dear. The means are insidious, but this is to be

expected from a serpent. Subterfuge is a tactical assumption in war—and make no mistake, this is a deadly war in which we are engaged. Cries of "That's not fair!" are meaningless on a battlefield.

Put on the armour of God, that you may be able to stand against the deceits of the devil.

For our wrestling is not against flesh and blood; but against principalities and powers, against the rulers of the world of this darkness, against the spirits of wickedness in the high places.

—Ephesians VI: 11-12

Satan has incited many scholars, first Protestant and now Catholic, to cast doubt on the integrity of the Genesis text itself. First, they play with the very word "she." They appeal to non-authorized codices such as the Septuagint, which was a translation of the Hebrew Scriptures into Alexandrian Greek by a group of Hellenistic Jews between 250 and 100 BC. In this version, the pronoun "he" is found in place of "she" in the second half of the *Protoevangelium:*

He shall crush thy head, and thou shalt lie in wait for *his* heel.

This, along with similar pleas to other ancient texts, has caused much confusion. While the use of "he" can certainly be interpreted to be a Messianic reference—"he" being the "seed" referred to in the previous line—the "woman" then becomes Eve, and the Marian message gets discarded.

Do not be fooled by those who say this is a trivial matter. We are not "splitting hairs." We walk on extremely unstable ground if we in any way diminish the importance of Mary in the history and culmination of Salvation. We become ...

> ... like a foolish man that built his house upon the sand,
>
> And the rain fell, and the floods came, and the winds blew, and they beat upon that house, and it fell, and great was the fall thereof.
>
> —Saint Matthew VII: 26-27

Another scholarly attack focuses on the actions "crush" and "lie in wait." The original Hebrew texts are of course lost to us, but as best as we can derive from copies, it is a fact that both verbs are represented by the same word,

$$\text{שׁוּף}$$

or *shuph.* It doesn't take an inordinate amount of research to discover that *shuph* has two meanings as do many words in English.

1. A by-form of ... *sha'aph* ... "to trample upon, crush"; Akkadian cognate *shapu,* "to trample underfoot"; Syriac. "to rub, wear out, bruise."

2. Arabic cognate *shapa,* "to see, look at, watch."
    —Thomas Mary Sennnott
    The Woman of Genesis

Nonetheless, our self-proclaimed experts seem to think they know more than St. Jerome about the nuances of these ancient languages, even though he was fifteen hundred years closer to them. Thus, under their scalpels, not only does "she" become "he" but the actions of both parties become the same:

He shall *bruise* thy head, and thou shalt *bruise* his heel.

The First Good News is thereby reduced from a promise of final victory to a description of an interminable battle, both sides merely injuring each other endlessly. The ramifications of these kinds of verbal switches are indeed profound.

In their zeal to denigrate the Word of God, liberal scholars and theologians have produced many "new" versions of the Bible, none of which rely on the Vulgate. Thus, pronouns and verbs swirling like so much confetti, we are bombarded with such travesties as:

And I will put enmity between thee and the woman, and between thy seed and her seed;
    it shall bruise thy head, and thou shalt bruise his heel.
    —*King James Version*

I will put enmity between you and the woman, and between your seed and her seed;

he shall bruise your head and you shall bruise his heel.
—*Revised Standard Version*
(Catholic Edition)

I will put enmity between you and the woman, and your seed and her seed:

He shall crush your head and you shall lie in wait for his heel.
—*Confraternity of Christian Doctrine*
(1962 Version)

I will put enmity between you and the woman, and between your offspring and hers;

He will strike at your head while you strike at his heel.[*]
—*New American Bible*

I will make you enemies of each other: you and the woman, your offspring and her offspring.

It will crush your head and you will strike at its heel.
—*The Jerusalem Bible*

From now on you and the woman will be enemies, as will all of your offspring and hers. And I will put the fear of you into the woman, and between your offspring and hers.

---

[*] A footnote suggests a better translation is "They will strike ... at their heels," but concedes the woman's offspring "primarily" is Jesus Christ.

He shall strike you on your head, while you will strike at his heel.

—The Living Bible

I will put enmity between you and the woman, and between your offspring and hers:

they shall strike at your head, and you shall strike at their heel.

—Tanakh: The (New) Jewish Bible

Enough! Enough of lies and half-truths which are worse! As Catholics struggling to understand and keep the Faith in these troubled times, we must remember that only one version of the Bible was ever declared to be the official text of the canonical Scriptures by a Council of the Church (Trent, 1546 AD) and free from error by a Pope (Pius XII in his encyclical letter *Divino Afflante Spiritu,* 1943): namely the old Latin Vulgate. Since the Douay-Rheims is the most faithful English translation to the Vulgate, we can read it without concern as to its integrity.

And there is more. Fortunately, we as Catholics are not subject to the banal whims of theologians and linguistic hacks. We are bound by an infinitely higher authority: the infallible teachings of the Roman Catholic Faith and Her Supreme Pontiffs. I refer here to the *infallible* papal definition of the Immaculate Conception made in 1854:

Hence, just as Christ, the Mediator between God and man, assuming human nature, blotted out the handwriting of the decree that stood against us, and fastening it triumphantly to the Cross, so the Most Holy Virgin, united with Him by a most intimate and indissoluble bond, was, with Him and through Him, eternally at enmity with the evil Serpent, and most completely triumphed over him, and thus crushed his head with her immaculate foot.

—Pope Pius IX
The bull *Ineffabilis Deus*

Thus, Mary is here identified as the one who crushes the serpent's head. Furthermore, we can also examine the *infallible* papal definition in 1950 of Our Lady's glorious Assumption:

We must remember especially that, since the second century, the Virgin Mary has been designated by the Holy Fathers as the new Eve, who, although subject to the new Adam, is most intimately associated with Him in that struggle against the infernal foe which, as foretold in the *Protoevangelium*, would finally result in that most complete victory over sin and death which are always associated in the writings of the Apostle of the Gentiles.

—Pope Pius XII
Munificentissimus Deus

Again, Mary is identified as the one foretold in the First Good News.

The final say, of course, should go to the Woman in question. In 1531, Our Lady appeared to Juan Diego in Mexico. She told him that She wished to be known as Our Lady of Guadalupe. Neither Juan, nor his shepherd, Bishop Zumarraga, understood the request. There was no town with the name Guadalupe near the site of the apparition, nor does the word have any meaning in Spanish. The most plausible explanation is that *de Guadalupe* sounds very similar to the Aztec *te coatlaxopeuh* (pronounced "te quatlasupe").

> *Te,* means "stone"; *coa* means "serpent"; *tha* is the noun ending which can be interpreted as "the"; while *xopeuh* means "crush" or "stamp out."
>
> —Thomas Mary Sennnott
> *The Woman of Genesis*

In other words, She wished to be called Our Lady Who Crushes the Stone Serpent—the "stone serpent" being the Aztec god to whom the Indians disemboweled thousands of men, women, and children on their altars of sacrifice every year. This ravenous serpent god was none other than the same serpent who slithered through the terrestrial paradise of Genesis. Within a decade of Our Lady's appearance to Juan Diego, nine million Indians converted to Catholicism, destroying the grip of the "stone serpent" on the lives of the Indians and reaffirming Her declaration of war against the enemy of mankind.

We must learn to stand firm against the subtle infiltrations of Satan. We must recognize his lies and bring them into the light of Truth where they perish. We must arrive at a place of trust with respect to the time-honored teachings of the Catholic Church.

With respect to the *Protoevangelium,* we need not be intimidated by the confusing musings of scholars who have lost their faith and wish to draw us into the vortex of their unbelief. Peter has spoken, the matter is closed. Mary has dotted the i's and crossed the t's. The only reliable rendering of Genesis III:15 is as follows:

> I will put enmities between thee and the woman, and thy seed and her seed:
> She shall crush thy head, and thou shalt lie in wait for her heel.
>
>   —*Douay Rheims Bible*

"Amen. So be it."

✝✝✝

6. PLAYING BEFORE HIM AT ALL TIMES

Holy Scripture was written for Mary, about Mary, and on account of Mary.

—Saint Bernard of Clairvaux

∞ ∞ ∞

Once we come to the realization that Mary the Mother of Jesus Christ is the "she" referred to in the *Protoevangelium,* and that She is also Wisdom Personified in the Book of Proverbs, a chain of stimulating Secrets concealed within the Sacred Scriptures throughout the ages begins to unwind like a well-spun mystery.

Before the world began, Mary was in the Mind of God. As He created the world, He was thinking of Her. When Adam and Eve fell, He held Her up to the serpent as a sign of Satan's ultimate destruction. As the complex twine of history unraveled, Mary remained foremost in His thoughts.

> I was with him forming all things: and was delighted every day, playing before him at all times.
> Playing in the world: and my delights were to be with the children of men.
>
> —Proverbs VIII: 30-31

Naturally, as the Holy Ghost "brooded" on His Spouse, awaiting the day when the most perfect of all creatures would fulfill Her destiny, She would emerge in His Revelation as He guided the hands and mouths of His prophets, "leaking out" between the lines and taking gradual form in the cascade of unfolding imagery.

Did the prophets who spoke the thoughts of God understand them? We cannot know for sure, but it is probable that they did not—at least, not fully. As the Spirit moved them, they obediently gave utterance. By His direction they preached to the people; through His inspiration they wrote it down. The specifics and ramifications of what they spoke and recorded would not become clear until the Light, Jesus Christ, came into the world to reveal them. Now, with the benefit of His illumination, we can retrace the thoughts of God as they unfolded throughout history. Here is where our journey becomes unbelievably exciting. We've already seen that "Ipsa"—Mary—marks the spot on our Treasure Map. Now let us trace the winding trail that leads us to Her, and through Her, to Her Son.

The Bible begins with the Act of Creation, when God formed the material universe out of the vacuum of absolute nothingness:

> In the beginning God created heaven, and earth.
> And the earth was void and empty, and darkness was upon the face of the deep; and the spirit of God moved over the waters.
>
> —Genesis I: 1-2

Yet, as we noted earlier, the Church understands that Mary was in the Mind of God even before this Beginning.

> The Lord possessed me in the beginning of his ways, before he made any thing from the beginning.
> I was set up from eternity, and of old before the earth was made.
> The depths were not as yet, and I was already conceived, neither had the fountains of waters as yet sprung out ...
> He had not yet made the earth, nor the rivers, nor the poles of the world.
> When he prepared the heavens, I was present ...
>
> —Proverbs VIII: 22-24, 26-27

The Hebrew form of Mary, *Miryam,* can be translated "exalted," "lady," "star," or "bitterness." When the Scriptures were first translated into Latin, the Church delighted in the similarity of "Maria" to *mare,* the sea. Do we really, after all our treks back to "square one," still believe in coincidences? Come now. God is in control. The connection of Mary and the sea goes all the way back to the very Act of Creation, long before Her name was Latinized.

When the Spirit of God moved over the waters, He was contemplating His Spouse. The Holy Ghost stirred the water, invigorating it in preparation for its eventual use in the Sacrament of Baptism. Furthermore, Mary would be the conduit through which Grace would enter the world in the Person of Her Divine Son. She therefore becomes absolutely necessary—in the immediate and personal sense—for each and every one of us, for without Her, none of us would have any hope of Salvation.

> The eternal Son of God, when He wished to assume the nature of man for the redemption and glory of man, and for this reason was about to enter upon a kind of mystic marriage with the entire human race, did not do this before He received the wholly free consent of His designated mother, who, in a way, played the part of the human race itself, according to the famous and truthful opinion of Aquinas: "Through the Annunciation the Virgin's consent was looked for in place of all human nature." Therefore, no less truly and properly may it be affirmed that nothing at all of the very great treasure of every grace, which the Lord confers, since "grace and truth came by Jesus Christ" [John I: 17], nothing is imparted to us except through Mary, God so willing; so just as no one can approach the highest Father except through the Son, so no one can approach Christ except through His Mother.
>
> —Pope Leo XIII
> The Encyclical, *"Octobri mense"*

Without Her obedient assent, He could not have entered our history, and so Grace would have been withheld from us. This is why she is called the Dispenser or Mediatrix of All Grace.

So, while She played in the Mind of God in the beginning, the Spirit moved over the waters, uniting Her with the process of Salvation. And this was only the beginning.

In the *Protoevangelium,* we learned that a certain Woman would have "seed." This unique Offspring would be the Messias. The first specific prophecy of the Savior, uttered by Balaam in the time of Moses, involved the rising of His "star":

> A STAR SHALL RISE out of Jacob, and a sceptre shall spring up from Israel ...
>
> —Numbers XXIV: 17

Some fifteen centuries later, this verse would draw Gaspar, Melchior, and Balthasar from Persia in search of the Messias.

> ... there came wise men from the east to Jerusalem.
>
> Saying, Where is he that is born king of the Jews? For we have seen his star in the east, and are come to adore him.
>
> —Saint Matthew II: 2

Since "Miryam" also means "star," Her destiny merges with His. Saints down through the centuries have celebrated Mary as the "Star of the Morning" and the "Star of the Sea."

> She is most beautifully likened to a star, for a star pours forth its light without losing anything of its nature. She gave us her Son without losing anything of her virginity. The glowing rays of a star take nothing away from its beauty. Neither has the Son taken anything away from his Mother's integrity.
>
> —Saint Bernard of Clairvaux

Seafarers navigate by the stars. So do we sinners steer with the aid of Mary's vigilant guidance. This beautiful imagery is further explained by Saint Thomas Aquinas:

> ... as mariners, in tempestuous weather, are guided by the star of the sea into port, so are souls guided by Mary over the sea of this world into Paradise.
>
> —Quoted by Saint Alphonsus de Liguori
> *The Glories of Mary*

For those of us wishing to increase our devotion to Our Blessed Mother, to access Her aid, or to better understand Mary's place in the scheme of things, there is perhaps no better meditation ever written than that of Saint Bernard:

> When you find yourself tossed by the raging storms of this great sea of life, far from land, keep your eyes fixed on this Star to avoid disaster. When the winds of tempta-

tion or the rocks of tribulation threaten, look up to the Star, call upon Mary!

When the waves of pride or ambition sweep over you, when the tide of detraction or jealousy runs against you, look up to the Star, call upon Mary! When the shipwreck of avarice, anger or lust seems imminent, call upon Mary!
—Saint Bernard of Clairvaux
Missus Est, II

Traditionally in mythology and literature the Morning Star is the planet Venus, the last light in the sky to grow pale and be absorbed by the growing brilliance of the rising sun. Small wonder, then, that Mary is described in the New Testament as …

A woman clothed with the sun, and the moon under her feet, and on her head a crown of twelve stars.
—The Apocalypse XII: 1

… and in the Old Testament as …

… she that cometh forth as the morning rising…
—Canticle of Canticles VI: 9

Ultimately, the title of Morning Star is claimed by Jesus Himself, when He triumphs at the end of time and all things come under His rule:

I am the Alpha and Omega, the first and the last, the beginning and the end …

I am the root and stock of David, the bright and morning star.

—The Apocalypse XXII: 13, 16

Thus we discover that the roles and attributes of Jesus and Mary become intimately intertwined in the Salvific Process, as well as in the history of the world. They are both the Morning Star. They are both heralds: She of Her Son, He of His Father.

We see this allusion throughout the Old Testament. For example, Mary's role as the Bearer of God is foreshadowed in the construction of the Ark of the Covenant:

Frame an ark of setim wood, the length whereof shall be of two cubits and a half: the breadth, a cubit and a half: the height, likewise, a cubit and a half.

And thou shalt overlay it with the purest gold within and without: and over it thou shalt make a golden crown round about ...

—Exodus XXV: 10-11

This box, made of extremely dense wood and completely plated inside and out with fine gold, was to house the Pentateuch, the Scrolls of Moses. It would be the visible focus of Hebrew worship, and the vessel upon which the *Shekinah* would descend.

The durable setim wood used in the Ark was seen by many Saints as a prefigurement of Mary's body, preserved from the corruption of Sin by virtue of Her Immaculate Conception, and from the corruption of

the grave by her Glorious Assumption.   The gold
represented the purity of Her soul, and the sanctity of
Her womb. Just as the Ark contained the Law, Mary
would contain the Lawgiver. Inside the Temple was a
shelf under which the Ark resided.   The shelf was
called the Propiatory or Mercy Seat. The quality of
Mercy has long been associated with the Virgin
Mary, especially by those Saints whose devotion to
Her was exemplary. For all these reasons and more
the Church has come to refer to Mary as the Ark of
the Convenant.

> Some of the Fathers have employed the words of the
> Psalmist: "Arise, O Lord, into thy resting place: thou and
> the ark, which thou hast sanctified" (Psalm 131: 8) and
> have looked upon the Ark of the Covenant, built of incor-
> ruptible wood and placed in the Lord's temple, as a type of
> the most pure body of the Virgin Mary, preserved and ex-
> empted from all corruption of the tomb and raised up to
> such glory in heaven.
>
> —Pope Pius XII
> *Munificentissimus Deus*

Just as the Ark was lined with gold, so was the
Temple built by Solomon in which it was housed:

> And the house before the oracle he overlaid with most
> pure gold, and fastened on the plates with nails of gold.
> And there was nothing in the temple that was not cov-
> ered with gold: the whole altar of the oracle he covered
> also with gold ...

And the floor of the house he also overlaid with gold within and without.

—III Kings VI: 21-22, 30

It follows, then, that another of Mary's many titles is the House of Gold.

Whether we consider the temple of portable tents which housed the Ark in the desert in the time of Moses, or the glorious edifice erected by Solomon that was the glory of Israel, the temple was the House of God.

Wisdom hath built herself a house …

—Proverbs IX: 1

As such, the temple was a prefigurement of the Mother of God, who would be the *Theotokos,* the God-Bearer. With this in mind, King David's prayer to God takes on a wealth of new meaning:

I have loved, O Lord, the beauty of thy house; and the place where thy glory dwelleth.

—Psalm XXV: 8

This is the same Psalm spoken by the priest during the Traditional Mass while he washes his hands at the conclusion of the Offertory:

I will wash my hands among the innocent; and will compass thy altar, O Lord:

That I may hear the voice of thy praise: and tell all thy wondrous works.

> I have loved, O Lord, the beauty of thy house; and
> the place where thy glory dwelleth ...
> —The Tridentine Mass

This connects Mary not only with the House of
God, but right into the heart of the Mass itself, the
Holy Sacrifice of Her Son on the altar. The priest, in
effect, says, "I have loved, O Lord, the beauty of
Your Mother, Mary." How sweet it is to bring Her
to mind, to consider Her comeliness, perfection, purity, holiness, and mercy, just before proceeding with
the Consecration.

Isn't it amazing how this all ties in together?

Mary hardly appeared at all in the first coming of Jesus
Christ in order that men, as yet but little instructed and
enlightened on the Person of her Son, should not remove
themselves from Him in attaching themselves too
strongly and too grossly to her. This would have appar-
ently taken place if she had been known ... The reasons
which moved the Holy Ghost to hide His spouse during
her life, and to reveal her but very little since the preaching of the Gospel, subsists no longer.

God, then, wishes to reveal and make known Mary, the
masterpiece of His hands, in these latter times:

1. Because she hid herself in this world and put herself
lower than the dust by her profound humility, having ob-
tained from God and from His Apostles and Evangelists
that she should not be made manifest.

2. Because, as she is the masterpiece of the hands of
God, as well here below by grace as in Heaven by glory,

He wishes to be glorified and praised in her by those who are living upon the earth.

3. As she is the dawn which precedes and reveals the Sun of Justice, who is Jesus Christ, she must be seen and recognized in order that Jesus Christ may also be.

4. Being the way by which Jesus came to us the first time, she will also be the way by which He will come the second time, though not in the same manner ...

—Saint Louis Marie de Montfort
True Devotion to Mary

Now—as if things weren't already interesting enough!—we pull back and flatten out a corner of our Treasure Map which has been curled over, concealing yet another Secret, a more perplexing mystery, an entirely unexpected aspect of the Mother of God. Here we read the words:

Mary: terrible as an army set in battle array.

One does not often see the name of the Blessed Virgin Mary beside the word "terrible." Indeed, most Catholics these days—those who most likely would not have come this far in our gallant expedition—are more used to thinking of Her as a benign maternal presence, a statue in the shadows in the back of the chapel holding a plump infant Jesus, or a relic of some forgotten time in the Church when such things as Motherhood and Chastity were more pertinent. Some have opted to turn Her into some kind of "earth mother," a newage* amalgam of Isis, Gaea, and Mother Nature. Some feminists have even tried to twist Her into a leathery parodic symbol of their warped sense of motorcycle-chain womanhood, the "first truly independent woman." All of which is sheer foolishness.

What is it about the audacious modern mind-set that so vainly encourages such pseudo-spiritual thumb-twiddling? How dare anyone so carelessly disregard the volumes and volumes of books, prayers, and meditations penned by Saints and honest scholars, Popes and prophets, men and women who devoted the entirety of their lives to learning and understand Mary's unique place in the scheme of things? Let us ignore these groundless speculations, and seek out Mary as She really is.

As we noted above, most people do not associate Mary with the word "terrible." Rather, we rightly honor Her and diligently hope to imitate Her in ...

> ... her profound humility, her lively faith, her blind obedience, her continual prayer, her universal mortification, her divine purity, her ardent charity, her heroic patience, her angelic sweetness and her divine wisdom. These are the ten principal virtues of the most holy Virgin.
>
> —Saint Louis Marie de Montfort
> *True Devotion to Mary*

---

* Newage: an intentional misspelling of "New Age" for rhyming purposes.

But there is another dimension to Her. Picture thousands of fierce men in polished armor, their swords sharpened, spears raised in salute, banners unfurled in the crisp breeze, shields blazing with piercing light as the sun rises over the field of battle—a powerful human machine geared and ready for war. Strong words, but they—no less than the gentle words above—describe Her to a tee:

Who is she that cometh forth as the morning rising,
fair as the moon, bright as the sun,
terrible as an army set in array?
—Canticle of Canticles VI: 9

The Canticle of Canticles in the Old Testament is a poetic book of heavenly mysteries. It was regarded by the Fathers as a description of the union between Christ and His beloved Church; and more specifically as the affection of Almighty God for perfect souls, every one of which He loves profoundly. Most specifically, and joyously, it is a song of the Triune God and His special Love and Devotion to the Immaculate and ever Virgin Mary.

All who have experienced love understand the profound and perplexing mixture of emotions displayed in this quotation from the Canticle of Canticles. She comes gently but inexorably, as slow and unstoppable as the dawn. She is passively beautiful, like the cool but steady moon which reflects the rays of the sun earthward. She is also actively beautiful like the sun, the radiant source of pure, blinding light. Moreover, as with all true lovers, She is awesome in the power that She wields, dreadful in Her fury, unquenchable in Her determination to please Her Spouse and to defend His honor.

Here we see again that Mary was "playing" before the Mind of God, like a melody that sometimes captures our imagination and delightfully goes on and on. She was the closest thing to Perfection He would ever create, and thus the Holy Ghost yearned for Her as time unfolded. Perhaps the relevance of the citation which crowns this chapter is now shimmering brilliantly:

> Holy Scripture was written for Mary, about Mary, and on account of Mary.
>
> —Saint Bernard of Clairvaux

No more clearly is this idea evident to the insightful eye than in the Canticle of Canticles, written centuries before Mary was physically born. Here the yearning of the Holy Ghost for His Spouse becomes manifested in the language of passionate Love:

> Who is this that cometh up from the desert, flowing with delights, leaning upon her beloved?
> ... Put me as a seal upon thy heart, as a seal upon thy arm, for love is strong as death, jealousy as hard as hell, the lamps thereof are fire and flames.

> Many waters cannot quench charity, neither can the floods drown it: if a man should give all the substance of his house for love, he shall despise it as nothing.
> —Canticle of Canticles VIII: 5, 6-7

Anyone who thinks that God is the least bit diminished when we give honor and devotion to His beloved Spouse has an incredibly small-minded idea of God and an atrophied perception of the power of Love—not to mention a nincompoopish lack of understanding regarding the wish every true Lover has that His Beloved be cherished and admired by all.

Furthermore, it is not maudlin to suggest that Jesus Christ cherishes His Mother: it is only *right*. Just because our ungracious, unceremonious generation has decided in its lust for self-gratification that motherhood is passé, there is certainly no reason to assume that God thinks likewise. Indeed, the carnal mind hasn't a clue about the deference and sincere regard God has for His Handmaid, Mother and Spouse. After all, Mary agreed to His indwelling, carried Him in Her womb, nourished Him at Her breast, clothed and fed Him as He grew up, witnessed His first miracle, stood by Him as He suffered on the Cross, and buried Him when the dreadful deed was done. Only a simpleton would think such holiness, obedience, and integrity on Her part would go unrewarded, uncherished, and unproclaimed. Only a fool or an ingrate would deem Her "just an incubator."

> ... it is an infallible mark of reprobation to have no es-
> teem and love for the holy Virgin; while on the other
> hand, it is an infallible mark of predestination to be en-
> tirely and truly devoted to her.
>
> —Saint Louis Marie de Montfort
> *True Devotion to Mary*

If ever there was a crime in this age, it has been the despicable dishonor paid this Woman by those who would deny Her the prominence that is rightly Hers. To think that the role of Mary in Salvation has been so downplayed, that Her Virginity has been called into question, that Her purity of heart should be so offended, and that devotion to Her has been offhandedly discounted by the butchers of the Faith.

This Woman, the brunt of so much vile and vehement hatred, is the humble Maiden who proclaimed:

> My soul doth magnify the Lord,
> And my spirit hath rejoiced in God my Savior.
>
> Because he hath regarded the humility of his handmaid;
> for behold from henceforth all generations shall call me
> blessed.
>
> Because he that is mighty, hath done great things to
> me; and holy is his name.
>
> —Saint Luke I: 46-49

Yes, since that time all generations have called Her "Blessed," including the current one—though our numbers have dwindled and our voices seldom manage to rise above the din of Her detractors, so outnumbered are we. May God have mercy on Her enemies, for just as She flies into battle for the honor of Her Lord, we can rest assured that the Holy Ghost who so yearned for Her throughout the ages, who took such delight in the very Idea of Her from the beginning, who in a very real sense "did it all for Her"—yes, Her Spouse will ride swiftly and with unspeakable ferocity to defend the Honor of His Lady.

Two guesses which side we want to be on.

Wait—what's this? As we let go of the flattened map it begins to curl up, and we see there is still *more* writing on the other side. How can this be? Is there no end to the avalanche that is Mary?

Happily, no.

> As the glorious Virgin Mary has been raised to the dignity of Mother of the King of kings, it is not without reason that the Church honors her, and wishes her to be honored by all, with the glorious title of Queen.
>
> —Saint Alphonsus Liguori
> *The Glories of Mary*

The titles, attributes, virtues, and accolades heaped upon the Blessed Virgin Mary never do end, for just as we think we've exhausted Her ongoing revelation in the Bible, we turn a page and find a whole new field ripe for harvest. And each time we think we have exhausted any given orchard, we glance over our shoulders as we pause to wipe our brows, and lo and behold the trees we thought were picked bare are again brimming with bright, colorful fruit, gleaming with the morning dew. Truly, it has been declared by many Marian Saints and scholars:

DE MARIA NUMQUAM SATIS
Of Mary, Never Enough

Indeed does it make sense, once we begin to fathom the Miracle that is Mary, to think otherwise? The same Holy Ghost who "brooded" on His Spouse throughout the Old Testament also inspires, activates, and spurs on the Holy Catholic Church up to the present. Small wonder that the Church has continued to ponder the Mother of God, and to diligently seek out Her many Graces, blessings, and positions within the framework of the Mystical Body of Christ.

Perhaps no greater summary of Our Lady's efforts can be found than the Litany of Loreto, which dates from the twelfth century in Italy (an Irish version goes back to the eighth), and which has been gradually enhanced by the additions of Popes along the way. May its recitation excite Her children to a deeper understanding of, and earnest devotion to, the Woman "playing before Him at all times," unto the consummation of all things.

∞ ∞ ∞

† † †

The Litany of Loreto
also known as
The Litany of the Blessed Virgin Mary

Lord, have mercy on us.
Christ, have mercy on us.
Lord, have mercy on us.
Christ hear us.
Christ, graciously hear us.
God the Father of Heaven, have mercy on us.
God the Son, Redeemer of the world, have mercy on us.
God the Holy Spirit, have mercy on us.
Holy Trinity, one God, have mercy on us.

Holy Mary, pray for us.
Holy Mother of God, pray for us.
Holy Virgin of virgins, pray for us.
Mother of Christ, pray for us.
Mother of divine grace, pray for us.
Mother most pure, pray for us.
Mother most chaste, pray for us.
Mother inviolate, pray for us.
Mother undefiled, pray for us.
Mother most amiable, pray for us.
Mother most admirable, pray for us.
Mother of good counsel, pray for us.
Mother of our Creator, pray for us.
Mother of our Savior, pray for us.

Virgin most prudent, pray for us.
Virgin most venerable, pray for us.
Virgin most renowned, pray for us.
Virgin most powerful, pray for us.
Virgin most merciful, pray for us.
Virgin most faithful, pray for us.

Mirror of justice, pray for us.
Seat of wisdom, pray for us.
Cause of our joy, pray for us.
Spiritual vessel, pray for us.
Vessel of honor, pray for us.
Singular vessel of devotion, pray for us.
Mystical rose, pray for us.
Tower of David, pray for us.
Tower of ivory, pray for us.
House of gold, pray for us.
Ark of the Covenant, pray for us.
Gate of heaven, pray for us.
Morning star, pray for us.
Health of the sick, pray for us.
Refuge of sinners, pray for us.
Comforter of the afflicted, pray for us.
Help of Christians, pray for us.

Queen of angels, pray for us.
Queen of patriarchs, pray for us.
Queen of prophets, pray for us.
Queen of Apostles, pray for us.
Queen of martyrs, pray for us.

Queen of confessors, pray for us.
Queen of virgins, pray for us.
Queen of all saints, pray for us.
Queen conceived without original sin, pray for us.
Queen assumed into heaven, pray for us.
Queen of the most holy Rosary, pray for us.
Queen of peace, pray for us.

Lamb of God, Who takest away the sins of the world,
    spare us O Lord.
Lamb of God, Who takest away the sins of the world,
    graciously hear us, O Lord.
Lamb of God, Who takest away the sins of the world,
    have mercy on us.

V/.   Pray for us, O holy Mother of God.

R/.   That we may be made worthy of the promises
       of Christ.

V/.   Let us pray.   Grant unto us, Thy servants, we
       beseech Thee, O Lord God, at all times to enjoy
       health of soul and body; and by the glorious
       intercession of Blessed Mary, ever virgin, when
       freed from the sorrows of this present life, to
       enter into that joy which hath no end.   Through
       Christ our Lord.

R/.   Amen.

7. COME OVER TO ME:
A MEDITATION

Mary, Our Blessed Mother, was the only creature in this world who never made Love shudder. You and I made Him shudder, but Mary never did.

—Virginia A. Kenny
Convent Boarding School

∞ ∞ ∞

Almost smack dab in the middle of my leather-bound Douay Bible, silently tucked away between the Book of Wisdom and the Prophecy of Isaias, is the Book of Ecclesiasticus. It was written in Hebrew two hundred years before the birth of Christ by a man named Jesus son of Sirach, and was translated into Greek by his grandson, also named Jesus. Though modern translations prefer the name Sirach for this book, the traditional name is far more illuminating as to its place in Catholic history. Ecclesiasticus, or "the Book of the Church," was once required reading for all catechumens—and with good reason.

The twenty-fourth chapter of this remarkable work provides us with a penetrating insight into the Miracle that is Mary. What I now write comes from the bottom of my heart, from the deepest recesses of my being. When the insanity of this age gets to me, as my feet slip on the loose and wobbly cobblestones, and the howl of the wind and the thrash of the hail unhinges my resolve, I take refuge in this beautiful and ancient prophecy. May its secrets and soothing unguents provide a healing elixir for you as well, and may we uphold one another as we continue on our wearying journey.

∞ ∞ ∞

WISDOM shall praise her own self, and shall be honoured in God, and shall glory in the midst of her people,

And shall open her mouth in the churches of the most High, and shall glorify herself in the sight of his power,

And in the midst of her own people shall be exalted, and shall be admired in the holy assembly.

—Ecclesiasticus XXIV: 1-3

WISDOM, who needs no further introduction, is here described in terms that resonate forward in time, pre-echoing the words She would one day say to Her cousin Elizabeth:

My soul doth magnify the Lord,
And my spirit hath rejoiced in God my Savior,

Because he hath regarded the humility of his handmaid; for behold from henceforth all generations shall call me blessed.

Because he that is mighty, hath done great things to me; and holy is his name.

—Saint Luke I: 46-49

True humility is the fruit of honest self-knowledge. Mary demonstrated the depths of Her humility by obeying God and offering Herself as the Vessel through which His Son would enter the world. This being accomplished, and thus sharing so intimately in the Love and Life of Our Savior, She is free to savor His Delight in Herself, and so rejoices in Her own exaltation. We who are corrupt cannot behave so because our sinfulness draws us inexorably toward selfish pride when we receive accolades. But Mary's humility is complete. When She rejoices in Herself, the glory goes straight to God. When we share in Her Joy, we honor Her and take our minds off our puny and prideful selves. Hence the Catholic Church exalts, praises, and admires Her in the Holy Assembly, and with great enthusiasm. It is right and just that we do so. And the laurels we heap upon Her pass through Her to God, for Her profound Humility renders Her absolutely Transparent. Nothing of our praise sticks to Her, but goes through Her to God.

And in the multitude of the elect she shall have praise, and among the blessed she shall be blessed, saying,

I came out of the mouth of the most High, the firstborn
before all creatures:

I made that in the heavens there should rise light that
never faileth, and as a cloud I covered all the earth:

I dwelt in the highest places, and my throne is in a pillar of a cloud.

—Ecclesiasticus XXIV: 4-7

Again we are confronted with the mystery of Mary
"playing before Him at all times," present in His
Mind as the world was created, foremost in His
Thoughts as He guided the Israelites out of Egypt.

And the Lord went before them to shew the way by day
in a pillar of a cloud, and by night in a pillar of fire ...

—Exodus XIII: 21

Next we come to a verse that, on the surface, is a
continuation of the same theme.

I alone have compassed the circuit of heaven, and have
penetrated into the bottom of the deep, and have walked in
the waves of the sea ...

—Ecclesiasticus XXIV: 8

Happily, we have had Saints who could see beyond
the obvious:

Fortunate, indeed, are the clients of this most compas-
sionate Mother; for not only does she succor them in this
world, but even in purgatory they are helped and comforted
by her protection. And as in that prison poor souls are in

the greatest need of assistance, since in their torments they cannot help themselves, our Mother of mercy does proportionately more to relieve them. St. Bernadine of Sienna says, "that in that prison, where souls that are spouses of Jesus Christ are detained, Mary has a certain dominion and plenitude of power, not only to relieve them, but even to deliver them from their pains."

And, first, with respect to the relief she gives. The same saint, in applying those words of Ecclesiasticus, *I have walked in the waves of the sea,* adds "that it is by visiting and relieving the necessities and torments of her clients, who are her children." He then says, "that the pains of purgatory are called waves, because they are transitory, unlike the pains of hell, which never end; and they are called waves of the sea, because they are so bitter. The clients of Mary, thus suffering, are often visited and relieved by her." "See, therefore," says Novarinus, "of what consequence it is to be the servant of this good Lady, for her servants she never forgets when they are suffering in those flames …"

—Saint Alphonsus de Liguori
The Glories of Mary

Knowing our own sinfulness and the extent of the evils we have committed throughout our lifetimes, the weight of our past offenses can sometimes drag us down into the dust. Purgatory looms—and in this we hope, for it is the detour with but one end, which is Heaven. Still, it is comforting to know that we will not be alone if, with God's help, we make it that far.

In any case, Mary not only played before the Mind of God before Her birth, but continued to do so in the minds of men afterwards. This splendid Lady sure does get around.

> I alone have compassed the circuit of heaven ...
> And have stood in all the earth: and in every people,
> And in every nation I have had the chief rule:
> And by my power I have trodden under my feet the hearts of all the high and low: and in these I sought rest, and I shall abide in the inheritance of the Lord.
>> —Ecclesiasticus XXIV: 8, 9-11

Yes, She has captured the hearts of kings and paupers, philosophers and merchants, knights and dolts, queens and flower girls. Small wonder the explorers named everything in sight after Mary, for She had trodden their valiant hearts under Her gentle feet, and rested tenderly within them.

Now we pause, take a deep breath, and let it out slowly, as we arrive at the crux:

> Then the creator of all things commanded, and said to me: and he that made me, rested in my tabernacle.
>> —Ecclesiasticus XXIV: 12

Around this revolves all else, that the God of all creation came and resided within Mary's very body; the very thought of which arouses our deepest gratitude, incites our most bewildered amazement, and enkindles our most profound hope. We can only imagine what it was like for Her, to realize that "He that made me rested in my tabernacle." We, who once in a great while snatch a flash of a glimpse of the beginnings of an insight when we receive Holy Communion, would do well to meditate on Her prolonged and intimate experience. Small wonder that Her soul magnified the Lord, that Her spirit rejoiced—and we continue to call Her "Blessed."

Indeed, many are the generations who will take delight in Her:

> And I took root in an honourable people, in the portion of my God his inheritance, and my abode is in the full assembly of saints.
>
> —Ecclesiasticus XXIV: 16

This fervor is then portrayed in blossoming imagery, reminiscent of the poetry of the Canticle of Canticles. One can easily get lost in the swirl of symbols and smells, the music of Love in bloom:

> I was exalted like a cedar in Libanus, and as a cypress tree on mount Sion.
>
> I was exalted like a palm tree in Cades, and as a rose plant in Jericho.
>
> As the fair olive tree in the plains, and as a plane tree by the water in the streets, I was exalted.
>
> I gave a sweet smell like cinnamon, and aromatical balm: I yielded a sweet odor like the best myrrh:
>
> And I perfumed my dwelling as storax, and galbanum, and onyx, and aloes, and as the frankincense not cut, and my odour is as the purest balm.

> I have stretched out my branches as the turpentine tree,
> and my branches are of honour and grace.
>
> —Ecclesiasticus XXIV: 17-22

A few verses further on, we come to a beautiful description of how closely Mary is intertwined with Her Son in purpose, mission, and intention. Here, also, is explained the delineation between them: how their paths differ. Would that more people hungering for the Truth would seek out, find, and devour these insightful passages:

> I am the mother of fair love, and of fear, and of knowledge, and of holy hope.
>
> —Ecclesiasticus XXIV: 24

How simple, and yet so complex, is Mary. As the Mother of Jesus, She is the Bearer of Love Personified. Within Her Son, and so within Herself, is knowledge and hope. In the course of time, after Her Son's Ascension, She would be present with the Apostles when the Holy Ghost descended upon them and the Catholic Church was born. Indeed, it was Her prayer that summoned Her Spouse on that occasion:

> Come, Holy Ghost, fill the hearts of Thy faithful and kindle in them the fire of Thy Love.
> Send forth Thy Spirit and they shall be created; and Thou shalt renew the face of the earth.

We would do well to recall that all Catholics used to be taught to pray for the gifts of the Holy Ghost: wisdom, understanding, counsel, fortitude, knowledge, piety, and—yes—*fear of the Lord.* Thus Mary, the "mother of fair love," is also the mother of rational, God-centered "fear." From these proceed "knowledge" and "holy hope."

> In me is all grace of the way and of the truth, in me is all hope of life and of virtue.
>
> —Ecclesiasticus XXIV: 25

How closely this prefigures the words of Her Son:

> I am the way, and the truth, and the life. No man cometh to the Father, but by me.
>
> —Saint John XIV: 6

But notice the subtle differences. Jesus would proclaim, *"I* am the way," whereas His Mother says, *"In me* is all grace of the way ..." Her claim is not to be the way itself, but by virtue of Grace, to be the harbinger, the precursor, the forerunner, the gateway, the bearer of Him who would be the way.

She continues:

> Come over to me, all ye that desire me, and be filled with my fruits.

For my spirit is sweet above honey, and my inheritance above honey and the honeycomb.

My memory is unto everlasting generations.

—Ecclesiasticus XXIV: 26-28

How much this resonates with, yet does not imitate, the words of Her Son:

Come to me, all you that labour, and are burdened, and I will refresh you.

Take up my yoke upon you, and learn of me, because I am meek, and humble of heart: and you shall find rest to your souls.

For my yoke is sweet and my burden light.

—Saint Matthew XI: 28-30

And then we read Her disclaimer, Her absolute denial that She in any way usurps the purpose or power of Her Son:

They that eat me, shall yet hunger: and they that drink me, shall yet thirst.

—Ecclesiasticus XXIV: 29

To feast on Mary is not enough, for She is not the end or the object of our worship. She cannot slake our thirst nor satisfy our hunger. She is but our means to Her Son, and the means by which He came to us. It is for Her Son and Him alone to fulfill our most fundamental needs:

I am the bread of life: he that cometh to me shall not
hunger: and he that believeth in me shall never thirst.
—Saint John VI: 35

Still, it is within Mary's power to grant favor to
those who do approach and appreciate Her; for after
all, no one desires our Salvation more than She
does—not even ourselves. She promises Her aid and
protection to those who earnestly seek Her help.

He that harkeneth to me, shall not be confounded: and
they that work by me, shall not sin.
—Ecclesiasticus XXIV: 30

This is why concerns about someone being "too
involved" or "preoccupied" with Mary are groundless. It is Her promise that they shall not be con-
fused. If they listen to Her, She will guide them. She
is, after all, Our Mother.

My reader will perhaps forgive me if I revel for a
moment in the next verse:

They that explain me shall have life everlasting.
—Ecclesiasticus XXIV: 31

I fully intend to make a career out of doing exactly
that. For those who are jealous, I make the following
suggestion wholeheartedly, and in the words of Her
Son:

Go, and do thou in like manner.

—Saint Luke X: 37

These proclamations of Mary as Wisdom Personified are not to be taken lightly. Today, more than
ever in history, we need to understand Her place in
the scheme of things, and Her pivotal importance in
our lives.

All these things are the book of life, and the covenant
of the most High, and the knowledge of the truth.

—Ecclesiasticus XXIV: 32

Mary is not "optional." These things which the
Holy Ghost revealed for our benefit through the hand
of Jesus son of Sirach in Ecclesiasticus, two centuries
before Mary was born, are all in the Book of Life.

And whoever was not found written in the book of life,
was cast into the pool of fire.

—The Apocalypse XX: 15

Those who deny the importance of Mary, or flee
from Her from lack of knowledge, deprive themselves
of a vast resource of strength and holiness, and thus
place themselves in great peril. We are called to follow the example of Christ Her Son, who was promised from the beginning, and whose line of descent
was carefully preserved in the Scriptures.

> Moses commanded a law in the precepts of justices, and an inheritance to the house of Jacob, and the promises of Israel.
>
> He appointed to David his servant to raise up of him a most mighty king ...
>
> —Ecclesiasticus XXIV: 33-34

Thus Moses promised through the Law that a mighty King would descend from David, who was Christ Our Lord ...

> Who filleth up wisdom as the Phison[*] and as the Tigris in the days of the new fruits.
>
> Who maketh understanding to abound as the Euphrates, who multiplieth it as the Jordan in the time of harvest.
>
> Who sendeth knowledge as light, and riseth up as Gehon in the time of the vintage.
>
> —Ecclesiasticus XXIV: 35-37

Within this beautiful prophecy is the sad realization that everyone will not seek out the help of His Mother:

> Who first hath perfect knowledge of her, and a weaker shall not search her out.

---

[*] The Phison is a river in Armenia which, like the Tigris, Euphrates, and Gehon, overflows its banks at the beginning of summer when the snow melts.

For her thoughts are more vast than the sea, and her
counsels more deep than the great ocean.
—Ecclesiasticus XXIV: 38-39

Again we find Mary's poetic connection with
mare, the sea. As Her virtues and attributes are indeed as vast and as intimidating as the ocean, many
will cringe in fear rather than embrace Her.
Undaunted, Wisdom flourishes, Her freely-given
Graces gushing forth in torrents of life-giving water.

I, wisdom, have poured out rivers.
I, like a brook out of a river of a mighty water; I like a
channel of a river and like an aqueduct, came out of paradise.
—Ecclesiasticus XXIV: 40-41

Ah, Mary! Again you remind us that You are the
promise made in Eden, the Woman of Genesis.

I said: I will water my garden of plants, and I will water
abundantly the fruits of my meadow.
And behold my brook became a great river, and my river
came near to the sea:
For I make doctrine shine forth to all as the morning
light, and I will declare it afar off.
—Ecclesiasticus XXIV: 42-44

Again you come forth …

> ... as the morning rising, fair as the moon, bright as the sun, terrible as an army set in array...
>
> —Canticle of Canticles VI: 9

... but this time armed with doctrine:

> And take unto you the helmet of salvation, and the sword of the spirit (which is the word of God).
>
> —Ephesians VI: 17

And in spite of our weakness, our cowardice, the end of our strength, and the limits of our understanding, You will come on and on, inexorably on. For as long as we sincerely seek the Truth, You will ferret us out and teach us with a Mother's tenacity, so that by Your patience and inexhaustible maternal ministrations we may come into full knowledge and holiness.

> I will penetrate to all the lower parts of the earth, and will behold all that sleep, and will enlighten all that hope in the Lord.
>
> I will yet pour out doctrine as prophecy, and will leave it to them that seek wisdom, and will not cease to instruct their offspring even to the holy age.
>
> See ye that I have not laboured for myself only, but for all that seek out the truth.
>
> —Ecclesiasticus XXIV: 45-47

No doubt all this talk of *doctrine* will be unsettling to those who prefer to make up their own religion as they go along—reflecting the modern tendency to remake God in man's image—but Mary's mission is rather to "them that seek wisdom," to "all that seek out the truth," and to "all that hope in the Lord."

And so it is with the glee of playful children, the gratitude of salvaged detritus, the humility of found-out sinners, the valor of an assembled army, and love of true admirers that we join our voices with Saints throughout the ages who have prayed:

> Hail, thou star of ocean
> God's own mother blest,
> Ever sinless Virgin,
> Gate of heavenly rest.
>
> Oh! by Gabriel's Ave,
> Uttered long ago,
> Eva's name reversing
> 'Stablish peace below.
>
> Break the captives' fetters,
> Light on blindness pour;
> All our ills expelling,
> Every bliss implore.
>
> Show thyself a Mother;
> May the Word divine,
> Born for us thine Infant,
> Hear our prayers through thine.
>
> Virgin all excelling,
> Mildest of the mild;

Freed from guilt preserve us
Meek and undefiled.

Keep our life all spotless,
Make our way secure,
Till we find in Jesus,
Joy for evermore.

Through the highest Heaven
To the almighty Three,
Father, Son and Spirit
One same glory be. Amen.

—"Ave Maria Stella"
The Raccolta

✝ ✝ ✝

8. FAR FROM ME: TOTAL CONSECRATION

Behold, I make all things new.

—The Apocalypse XXI: 5

∞ ∞ ∞

Having considered the Blessed Virgin Mary for the last seven chapters—indeed, we could go on for seventy times seventy times seven volumes and still only skim the gently rolling surface of the Marian Sea—there comes a juncture when we need to plan a course of action. Knowledge that is not put to use is like fruit left on a tree to wither and fall to the ground. Now that we have come to a clearer realization of the awesome power and position of the Mother of God, what are we going to do about it?—about Her?—about us in relation to Her?

Mary, as we have seen, is the most perfect creature God ever made, more glorious than all the Angels put together, more pleasing to Him than all the Saints combined. It therefore stands to reason that if we

wish to be pleasing to Him, we would do well to imitate Her. When we attach and devote ourselves to the
Mother of God, She in turn takes an interest in us.
More than an interest, She has a Mother's deep and
abiding concern for Her children, wanting what is
holiest and best for them. She desires our Salvation
more than we do for ourselves.

> When Mary has struck her roots in a soul, she produces
> there marvels of grace, which she alone can produce, be-
> cause she alone is the fruitful Virgin who never has had,
> and never will have, her equal in purity and fruitfulness.
> —Saint Louis Marie de Montfort
> *True Devotion to Mary*

The most perfect way that we can attach ourselves
to Our Lady is called the Total Consecration. While
this has been practiced in one form or another over
the centuries by various Saints, the best and most
precise formulation was conceived by Saint Louis de
Montfort, whose feast day is April 28.

Louis Marie Grignion de la Bachelaraie was born
in the town of Montfort-la-Canne in Brittany in 1673.
After his ordination in 1700, he became a traveling
missionary, wandering through France, which was
falling under the shadow of the Jansenist heresy.
Jansenism was a joy-killing severity-instilling Cal-
vinist-resembling hyper-puritanism which had been
condemned by the Church twice before Louis' birth,
yet continued to thrive in France. It is amazing how
people will opt for a merciless parody of God's

Revelation rather than accept with joy and thanksgiving the profound Mercy He expressed in the Person of His Son. It's sort of the spiritual version of walking around with a sign on one's back that says, "Kick me."

In any case, three hundred years ago, reverence to Our Lady was on the decline as a result of the Jansenist influence, and Louis met with serious opposition as he traveled through France, preaching devotion to Her. His stiffest opposition came from, of all people, the bishops and clergy. Discouraged by their antagonism toward his message, Louis took his case to Pope Clement XI, asking whether he was doing something wrong. The Pope told him to continue his efforts, appointing him Missionary Apostolic, and—as is always the quirk and challenge of Catholicism—instructed him to work under obedience to the diocesan authorities. This Louis did until his death in 1716. He was canonized in 1947.

Of Saint de Montfort's numerous works, his most important was *True Devotion to Mary.* This book is *required reading* for all Catholics who want to understand Mary's proper place with respect to our Salvation, and it provides the best course for nurturing and achieving a deep and abiding relationship with Her. It is also a *survival guide* for the Faithful in times of persecution. The Saint understood the importance of his book, for within its pages he prophesied:

I clearly foresee that raging beasts shall come in fury to tear with their diabolical teeth this little writing and him whom the Holy Ghost has made use of to write it—or at least to smother it in the darkness and silence of a coffer, that it may not appear. They shall even attack and persecute those who shall read it and carry it out in practice.

—Saint Louis Marie de Montfort
True Devotion to Mary

As it turned out, the religious order he founded was severely persecuted, and the manuscript itself was lost for a hundred years. It was found by accident in 1842, which is providential for us since it seems eerily directed to our generation in particular:

Mary must shine forth more than ever in mercy, in might and in grace, in these latter times: in mercy, to bring back and lovingly receive the poor strayed sinners who shall be converted and shall return to the Catholic Church; in might, against the enemies of God, idolaters, schismatics, Mahometans, Jews and souls hardened in impiety, who shall rise in terrible revolt against God to seduce all those who shall oppose them and to make them fall by promises and threats; and finally, she must shine forth in grace, in order to animate and sustain the valiant soldiers and faithful servants of Jesus Christ, who shall battle for His interests.

And lastly, Mary must be terrible to the devil and his crew, as an army ranged in battle, principally in these latter times, because the devil, knowing that he has but little time, and now less than ever, to destroy souls, will every day redouble his efforts and his combats. He will presently raise up cruel persecutions and will put terrible snares before the faithful servants and true children of Mary, whom it gives him more trouble to conquer than it does to conquer others.

—Saint Louis Marie de Montfort
True Devotion to Mary

When anyone says to me, "I'm on a limited budget; what books do I absolutely *need* to buy?" my recommendations are: 1) the Douay-Rheims Bible, preferably the edition with the Haydock footnotes if they can possibly swing it, and 2) *True Devotion to Mary.* "Once you're consecrated to Her," I explain, "you can trust Her to lead you to whatever else you need."

First off, we as Faithful Catholics need to recognize and get it through our heads that the whole Protestant buzz over "Catholics put too much emphasis on Mary" is silly. We should render such nonsense the response it deserves: since it demonstrates their *ignorance,* we should *ignore* it. Truly, we should know and proclaim that *De Maria numquam satis—of Mary, there is never enough!* How can we overemphasize that which is so magnificent and awesome as to be beyond comprehension? When we come to realize that ...

In this Queen alone are comprehended and contained more treasures than in all the rest of things joined together, and the variety and preciousness of her riches

honor the Lord above all the multitudes of the other
creatures.

> —Sister Mary of Jesus of Agreda
> "The Conception"
> *Mystical City of God*

… what would be the sense of minimizing Her
splendor? To do anything but magnify Mary, to
shower Her with praise and devotion, is to behave
irrationally. Besides, if the Protestants put so much
stock in the Bible, and …

> Holy Scripture was written for Mary, about Mary,
> and on account of Mary.
>
> —Saint Bernard of Clairvaux

… then what's their problem? Enough of this. Let
us move on to something sensible, reasonable, and
certainly more constructive.

Secondly, we need to recognize, as so many Saints
have told us, that we absolutely *need* Mary. There is
nothing *optional* about this, there is no room for personal opinion on the matter. It is *de Fide*—of the
Faith—so we must accept it. Listen to the declara-
tions of great and holy Saints:

> No one can enter into Heaven except through Mary, as
> entering through a gate … No one ever finds Christ but
> with and through Mary. Whoever seeks Christ apart from
> Mary seeks Him in vain.
>
> —Saint Bonaventure

The salvation of everyone is left to the care of this Blessed Virgin.

—Saint Peter Damian

Mary is called "The Gate of Heaven" because no one can enter Heaven but through her means.

—Saint Alphonsus de Liguori

Sinners receive pardon by the intercession of Mary alone.

—Saint John Chrysostom

All gifts, virtues, and graces of the Holy Ghost are administered by the hands of Mary to whomever she desires, when she desires, and in the manner she desires, and to whatever degree she desires.

—Saint Bernadine of Siena

All the saints have a great devotion to Our Lady: no grace comes from Heaven without passing through her hands. We cannot go into a house without speaking to the doorkeeper. Well, the Holy Virgin is the doorkeeper of Heaven.

—Saint John Mary Vianney, the Curé of Ars

O Most Holy Virgin, receive us under thy protection if thou wouldst see us saved, for we have no hope of salvation but through thy means.

—Saint Ephrem

Whoever honors, loves, serves and invokes Mary with humility and confidence will ascend to Paradise.

—Saint John Eudes

No one, not even a sinner, who devoutly recommends himself to her shall ever become the prey of Hell.

—Saint Catherine of Siena

Unless the prayers of Mary interposed, there could be no hope of mercy.

—Saint Bridget of Sweden

For, since it is the will of Divine Providence that we should have the God-Man through Mary, there is no other way for us to receive Christ except from her hands.

—Saint Pope Pius X

—All the above quotes are from
The Apostolic Digest
Edited by Michael Malone

Yes, yes, we know very well what Protestants have to say about "one mediator," but as we saw earlier, Catholics have a different and far more logical perspective:

> Therefore, no less truly and properly may it be affirmed that nothing at all of the very great treasure of every grace, which the Lord confers, since "grace and truth came by Jesus Christ" [John I: 17], nothing is imparted to us except through Mary, God so willing; so just as no one can approach the highest Father except through the Son, so no one can approach Christ except through His Mother.
>
> —Pope Leo XIII
> The Encyclical, *"Octobri mense"*

The fact is that to the degree they close themselves off from Mary, so much do they also imperil their own Salvation.

Thirdly, we need to foster devotion within ourselves to the Blessed Virgin Mary. Genuine devotion to Our Lady begins with admiration of Her greatness. The more we learn about Her, the more we are awed by all that She is. Small wonder that God took so much delight in Her throughout the ages. Admiration naturally leads to imitation, the desire to foster within ourselves the virtues we find so admirable in Her. Truly, Mary furnishes the perfect model for the life of every person, regardless of age, sex, occupation, or vocation. There is no human being who cannot benefit from mirroring Mary. The trouble is that there is no way that we can accomplish it on our own, because we are thoroughly rotten due to Original Sin. Therefore we must invoke Her intercession, ask Her to give us the Grace and Guidance to make our imitation of Her genuine and complete. On Her assistance and cooperation we can fully depend, for She loves us as Her own, and longs to bring forth Christ in us, and us in Christ.

Fourthly, we need to dedicate ourselves totally and completely to Her. We need to learn all we can about the Total Consecration, and then do it. Simple.

All our perfection consists in being conformed, united and consecrated to Jesus Christ; and therefore the most perfect of all devotions is, without any doubt, that which the most perfectly conforms, unites, and consecrates us to Jesus Christ. Now, Mary, being the most conformed of all creatures to Jesus Christ, it follows that, of all devotions, that which most consecrates and conforms the soul to Our Lord is devotion to His holy Mother, and that the more a soul is consecrated to Mary, the more it is consecrated to Jesus.

Hence it comes to pass that the most perfect consecration to Jesus Christ is nothing else but a perfect and entire consecration of ourselves to the Blessed Virgin, and this is the devotion I teach; or, in other words, a perfect renewal of the vows and promises of Holy Baptism.

This devotion consists, then, in giving ourselves entirely to Our Lady, in order to belong entirely to Jesus through her. We must give her (1) our body, with all its senses and its members; (2) our soul, with all its powers; (3) our exterior goods of fortune, whether present or to come; (4) our interior and spiritual goods, which are our merits and virtues, and our good works, past, present, and future. In a word, we must give her all we have in order of nature and in order of grace, and all that may become ours in the future, in the orders of nature, grace and glory; and this we must do without reserve of so much as one farthing, one hair, or one least good action; and we must do it also for all eternity; and we must do it, further, without pretending to, or hoping for, any other recompense for our offering and service except the honor of belonging to Jesus Christ through and in Mary—as though that sweet Mistress were not (as she always is) the most generous and the most grateful of creatures.

—Saint Louis Marie de Montfort
True Devotion to Mary

In other words, in giving Her everything internal and external that we would ever precede with the possessive pronoun "my," we offer ourselves as slaves to Mary. *"Slaves?!?!?!"* Yes, the word rankles, grates against our sensibilities, sends shivers up and down our spines, makes us want to close the book and turn on the television or reach for a scotch. Well, leave the TV off—the scotch is optional, but don't overdo it. This is indeed a hard thing to swallow, but we mustn't make the mistake of turning away from a great blessing just because we are uncomfortable with the terminology. The word "slave" is indeed disturbing—especially here in the United States of America—but it is not foreign to Catholicism, nor does Jesus ever ask of us something which He wasn't willing to do Himself:

There is nothing among men which makes us belong to one another more than slavery. There is nothing among Christians which makes us more absolutely belong to Jesus Christ and His holy Mother than the slavery of the will, according to the example of Jesus Christ Himself, who took on Himself the form of a slave for love of us (*Phil.* 2:7); and also according to the example of the holy Virgin, who called herself the servant and slave of the Lord. (*Lk.* 1:38) ...

Before Baptism we were slaves of the devil. Baptism has made us the slaves of Jesus Christ: Christians must needs be either the slaves of the devil or the slaves of Jesus Christ.

—Saint Louis Marie de Montfort
True Devotion to Mary

Willing slavery—consciously choosing to bind oneself to the service of another—is not all that unfamiliar to us. Marriage, in its truest Sacramental form, is much the same thing. The difference in the Total Consecration is that, unlike marriage in which commitment is made to a spouse until death, we are freely chaining ourselves to the Mother of Fair Love for all eternity. If we have learned anything in the last few chapters, it is that Mary is well worth cherishing, admiring, honoring, and imitating. Making the Total Consecration attaches us to Her in a solemn promise of fealty and love.

According to Saint Louis de Montfort's prescription, we prepare for the Consecration over a period of thirty-three days. For each day he suggests a reading

from Scripture or the *Imitation of Christ* by Thomas
à Kempis, followed by prayers that help to properly
direct our thoughts and intentions; prayers such as:

Saint Louis de Montfort's
Prayer to Jesus

O most loving Jesus, deign to let me pour forth my
gratitude before Thee, for the grace Thou hast bestowed
upon me in giving me to Thy holy Mother through the
devotion of Holy Bondage[*], that she may be my advocate
in the presence of Thy majesty and my support in my ex-
treme misery. Alas, O Lord! I am so wretched that without this dear Mother I should be certainly lost. Yes, Mary
is necessary for me at Thy side and everywhere: that she
may appease Thy just wrath, because I have so offended
Thee; that she may save me from the eternal punishment
of Thy justice, which I deserve; that she may contemplate
Thee, speak to Thee, pray to Thee, approach Thee and
please Thee; that she may help me to save my soul and
the souls of others; in short, Mary is necessary for me
that I may always do Thy holy will and seek Thy greater
glory in all things. Ah, would that I could proclaim
throughout the whole world the mercy that Thou hast

---

[*] It is no coincidence that the concept of "bondage" has a warped
pornographic connotation in our culture. Satan's efforts against
all things Marian have been rampant and insidious for a long,
long, time. Understanding this, we mustn't allow ourselves to be
swayed from our course by a mere dislike or misinterpretation of
certain words.

shown to me! Would that everyone might know I should be already damned, were it not for Mary! Would that I might offer worthy thanksgiving for so great a blessing! Mary is in me. Oh, what a treasure! Oh, what a consolation! And shall I not be entirely hers? Oh, what ingratitude! My dear Savior, send me death rather than such a calamity, for I would rather die than live without belonging entirely to Mary. With St. John the Evangelist at the foot of the cross, I have taken her a thousand times for my own and as many times have given myself to her; but if I have not yet done it as Thou, dear Jesus, dost wish, I now renew this offering as Thou desire me to renew it. And if Thou seest in my soul or my body anything that does not belong to this august princess, I pray Thee to take it and cast it far from me, for whatever in me does not belong to Mary is unworthy of Thee.

O Holy Spirit, grant me all these graces. Plant in my soul the Tree of Life, which is Mary; cultivate it and tend it so that it may grow and blossom and bring forth the fruit of life in abundance. O Holy Spirit, give me great devotion to Mary, Thy faithful spouse; give me great confidence in her maternal heart and an abiding refuge in her mercy, so that by her Thou mayest truly form in me Jesus Christ, great and mighty, unto the fullness of His perfect age. Amen.

—Saint Louis Marie de Montfort
True Devotion to Mary

... or ...

Saint Louis de Montfort's
Prayer to Mary

Hail Mary, beloved Daughter of the Eternal Father. Hail Mary, admirable Mother of the Son. Hail Mary, faithful Spouse of the Holy Ghost. Hail Mary, my Mother, my loving Mistress, my powerful sovereign. Hail, my joy, my glory, my heart and my soul. Thou art all mine by mercy, and I am thine by justice. But I am not yet sufficiently thine. I now give myself wholly to thee without keeping anything back for myself or others. If thou seest anything in me which does not belong to thee, I beseech thee to take it and make thyself the absolute Mistress of all that is mine. Destroy in me all that may displease God; root it up and bring it to nought; place and cultivate in me everything that is pleasing to thee.

May the light of thy faith dispel the darkness of my mind; may thy profound humility take the place of my pride; may thy sublime contemplation check the distractions of my wandering imagination; may thy continuous sight of God fill my memory with His presence; may the burning love of thy heart inflame the lukewarmness of mine; may thy virtues take the place of my sins; may thy merits be my only adornment in the sight of God and make up for all that is wanting in me. Finally, dearly beloved Mother, grant if it be possible, that I may have no other spirit but thine to know Jesus, and His Divine Will; that I have no other soul but thine to praise and glorify God; that I may have no other heart but thine to love God with a love as pure and ardent as thine. I do not ask thee for visions, revelations, sensible devotion or spiritual pleasures. It is thy privilege to see God clearly; it is thy privilege to enjoy His heavenly bliss; it is thy privilege to triumph gloriously in Heaven at the right hand of thy Son and to hold absolute sway over angels, men and demons; it is thy privilege to dispose of all the gifts of God, just as thou willest.

Such is, O heavenly Mary, the "best part," which the Lord has given thee and which shall never be taken away from thee—and this thought fills my heart with joy. As for my part here below, I wish for no other than that which was thine: to believe sincerely without spiritual pleasures; to suffer joyfully without human consolation; to die continually to myself without respite; and to work zealously and unselfishly for thee until death as the humblest of thy servants. The only grace I beg thee to obtain for me is that every day and every moment of my life I may say: Amen, so be it—to all that thou didst do while on earth; Amen, so be it—to all thou art now doing in Heaven; Amen, so be it—to all that thou art doing in my soul, so that thou alone mayest fully glorify Jesus in me for time and eternity. Amen.

—Saint Louis Marie de Montfort
True Devotion to Mary

Then, on the thirty-fourth day—it is recommended that we plan ahead so that this day falls on one of Our Lady's Feast Days—having made a good Confession, we receive Holy Communion, and then make our formal pledge to do all our actions ...

... by Mary, with Mary, in Mary, and for Mary. So
that we may do them all the more perfectly by Jesus, with
Jesus, in Jesus, and for Jesus.

—Saint Louis Marie de Montfort
True Devotion to Mary

Simple, really. From that moment on, we hand the
keys to Mary and let Her slip into the driver's seat of
our lives. Since She knows the Way to Heaven only
too well, we can be confident in Her sense of direction. It's something of a relief, too, when we realize
even more fully than ever that our lives are not our
own. In this sense the total honesty of the Consecration is most satisfying.

Before we conclude, I wish to advise my readers
and friends of several important things:

First, I have yet to meet a person who made the
Total Consecration who did not derive enormous
benefit from it. To a man, to a woman, everyone ex-
periences a radical change in their spiritual lives for
the better.

Second, Mary will turn our lives inside out and up-
side down. Our Blessed Mother wants us to be
pleasing to Her Son, and pleasing She shall make us.
We all tend to build monuments to ourselves, often
without realizing it. Many of us have erected majestic
cathedrals in our own honor. When we commit ourselves to Mary, She will bring in the bulldozers and
level such monstrosities. So we rebuild, this time
taking care to raise our monument to God.   Of
course, old habits die hard, and so we think we can

get away with adding a side chapel dedicated to ourselves; in which case Mary does another bulldozer sweep. This process is agonizing and requires patience, and at times we may wish She would stop handing us roses thorns first, but once we are Hers we can rest assured that everything that happens thereafter is all the more for our good.

Third—and this too, is universal—during the thirty-three days of preparation, we will go through periods of depression, often accompanied by situations that incite tension or personal difficulty. Our lives may seem to unravel before our very eyes. When this began to happen in my life, I told the person who had recommended the Total Consecration to me. She responded sweetly, "Oh yes, I forgot to warn you …"

So I am warning you, my devout readers: be prepared. As we approach Mary who is so perfect, so pure, so radiantly humble, yet so stunning and playfully delightful, our own impurity, imperfection, and sinfulness can get terribly gnarly by contrast. It can be exasperating, and certainly humiliating, but it is nonetheless purifying; and we do well to endure it with patience and hope. Hang in there. She will get you through.

Now we will roll up our Treasure Map, for having found the Cache of Gold, we must pass on the Directions to others so that they, too, may find this precious Trove. As for ourselves, "Ipsa"—the "X" that marks the spot—is now part of us, for the "spot" She marks is deep within our hearts.

And now, refreshed and renewed, and so much richer, we set sail for the next great adventure …

AFTERWORD

BY

CHARLES A. COULOMBE

She shall crush thy head, and thou shalt lie in wait
for her heel.

—Genesis III: 15

∞ ∞ ∞

The book that you have just read is an important
one for a number of reasons. The most important is
that it puts Mary right back in the center of things
where She belongs. After forty years of pop theologians warning dourly about "Mary Maximalists,"
and such standard textbooks as *Christ Among Us*
solemnly telling us that Marian devotion is "relevant
to some, particularly older, Catholics," Mr. Biersach's book has been a breath of fresh air. "No," it
tells us, "if you will not take the Mother, you cannot
have the Son."

This is an extremely important reminder of objective reality, in a sphere where Unitarian subjectivism has become the norm, whatever denominational name one applies. Not only is Mary optional, so too is Jesus. Be nice, and all will be well. What the first Protestants (although not Martin Luther, as it happens), did not realize was that the opposite of the dictum just cited is also true: get rid of the Mother, and you will get rid of the Son. And so they have, at least in the mainstream denominations.

But Mr. Biersach does not just leave us with this truth, he leaves us with several others. Key is the implication that Mary is indeed the root of all or most that is decent in our lives. This is in keeping with J. R. R. Tolkien's declaration that all he knew of beauty was derived from Our Lady.

Every age has elements of sanity, and of insanity. In our time, the latter seems particularly dominant. But you have just had the privilege of reading a book that is refreshingly, incredibly, sane.

—Charles A. Coulombe
Arcadia, California
June 25, 2002
The Feast of St. William the Abbot (1142 AD)

AUTHOR'S NOTE

Dear Reader,

I hope the information contained in this book has been of help to you. My intention was to spark the imagination and pique your curiosity, to start you on your journey as it were. I purposely avoided detailed footnotes in the hope that, instead of looking up specific sentences, the inquisitive will read entire books that were written by men and women of greater skill, keener insight, and more profound Faith than myself. May your quest be as stimulating and fruitful as my own.

Those who enjoyed the first edition of this book will find that I changed only a few words, corrected a sprinkling of typos, added a couple of magnificent quotations from Saint Anselm, and appended a short section of favorite Marian prayers. This enlarged format also allowed me to present the complete Consecration prayers of Saint Louis Marie de Montfort without resorting to the use of ellipses.

I wish to express my gratitude to Bill Feeney and the folks at Catholic Treasures for publishing this work, and to Jeannette Coyne without whose generosity this new edition would not have been possible—please keep her and her family in your prayers. Thanks also to those dedicated Catholics who helped me to discover the wonders of the Blessed Mother upon my return to the Faith: Phyllis Schabow, Thomas Zola, Father Robert Bishop, CMF, Brother Leonard Mary, MICM, Brother Thomas Aquinas, MICM, and a special Novena to Michael Malone whose passing has left such a gaping crater—I miss him terribly and hope we meet again one of these days.

As for my good friends, Charles A. Coulombe and Mark Alessio, words cannot convey my appreciation for their own meritorious labors reintroducing Catholics to their own religion, nor for their humbling thoughts expressed in the foreword and afterword of this volume.

I also wish to raise my glass to Saint Philip Neri, "the Laughing Saint," on whose Feast Day I was born, and whose unshakable wit and spirit have influenced my life and my writing throughout the years.

Finally, may I meld myself with a great Saint in his superbly-worded request:

> Devout reader, should this work, as I trust it will, prove acceptable to you, I beg that you will recommend me to

the Blessed Virgin, that she may give me great confidence in her protection. Ask this grace for me; and I promise you, whoever you may be, that I will ask the same for you who do me this charity. O blessed are they who bind themselves with love and confidence to these two anchors of salvation, Jesus and Mary. Certainly, they will not be lost.

—Saint Alphonsus Liguori
The Glories of Mary

God bless you all, and Mary keep you.

—William L. Biersach
Rock Haven
June 27, 2002
The Feast of Saint Cyril of Alexandria (444 AD)
"The Soul of the Council of Ephesus,"
who contributed the phrase
"Holy Mary, Mother of God, pray for us sinners"
to the Hail Mary.

✝✝✝

APPENDIX:
MARIAN PRAYERS

AVE MARIA

HAIL MARY, full of grace, the Lord is with Thee. Blessed art Thou among women, and blessed is the fruit of Thy womb, Jesus. Holy Mary, Mother of God, pray for us sinners now and at the hour of our death. Amen.

SALVE REGINA

HAIL HOLY QUEEN, Mother of Mercy, hail, our life, our sweetness, and our hope. To Thee do we cry, poor banished children of Eve; to Thee do we send up our sighs, mourning and weeping in this vale of tears. Turn then, most gracious Advocate, Thine eyes of mercy toward us, and after this our exile, show unto us the blessed fruit of Thy womb, Jesus. O clement, O loving, O sweet Virgin mary!

SUB TUUM PRAESIDIUM

WE FLY TO THY PATRONAGE, O holy Mother of God; despise not our petitions in our necessities, but deliver us always from all dangers, O glorious and blessed Virgin. Amen.

AVE REGINA CÆLORUM

HAIL, O QUEEN OF HEAVEN enthroned!
Hail, by Angels Mistress owned!
Root of Jesse, Gate of morn,
Whence the world's true Light was born:

Glorious Virgin, joy to Thee,
Loveliest whom in Heaven they see:
Fairest Thou where all are fair,
Please with Christ our songs to spare.

PRAYER TO OUR LADY OF GUADALUPE

OUR LADY OF GUADALUPE, Mystical Rose, make intercession for Holy Church, protect the Sovereign Pontiff, help all those who invoke Thee in their necessities, and since Thou art the ever Virgin Mary and Mother of the True God, obtain for us from Thy most holy Son the grace of keeping our Faith, sweet hope in the midst of the bitterness of life, burning charity and the precious gift of final perseverance. Amen.

PRAYER IN TIME OF TEMPTATION

By Thine Immaculate Conception, O Mary, make my body pure, and make my soul holy. My Mother, preserve me this day(night) from mortal sin. Amen.

THE ANGELUS

V/. THE ANGEL of the Lord declared unto Mary.
R/. And she conceived by the Holy Ghost.

Hail Mary ...

V/. Behold the handmaid of the Lord.
R/. Let it be done unto me according to Thy word.

Hail Mary ...

V/. (Genuflect) And the Word was made flesh,
R/. And dwelt among us.

Hail Mary ...

V/. Pray for us, O holy Mother of God,
R/. That we may be made worthy of the promises of Christ.

Let us pray. Pour forth, we beseech Thee, O Lord, Thy grace into our hearts; that we, to whom the Incarnation of Christ Thy Son, was made known by the message of an Angel, may by His Passion and Cross be brought to the glory of His Resurrection. Through Christ our Lord. Amen.

—To be said at dawn, noon, and eventide
throughout the year.

THE REGINA CÆLI

QUEEN OF HEAVEN, rejoice! Allelulia.
For He Whom Thou didn't merit to bear, Alleluia.
Hath risen, as He said. Alleluia.
Pray for us to God. Alleluia.
V/. Rejoice and be glad, O Virgin Mary, Alleluia.
R/. Because the Lord is truly risen. Alleluia

> —To be said in place of The Angelus
> during Eastertide.

INVOCATIONS

Mother of Perpetual Help, pray for us.

Sweet Heart of Mary, be my Salvation.

O Heart most pure of the Blessed Virgin Mary, obtain for me from Jesus a pure and humble heart.

Immaculate Queen of Peace, pray for us.

O Mary, conceived without sin, pray for us who have recourse to Thee.

† † †